I0166351

A Reconciliation Reader-Retreat: Read-Aloud Lessons, Stories, and Poems for Young Catholics Preparing for Confession

Compiled and Edited by
Janet P. McKenzie

A RACE for Heaven Product

Biblio Resource Publications
108½ South Moore Street
Bessemer, MI 49911
2011

©2011 by Janet P. McKenzie

All right reserved. No part of this book may be reproduced, stored in a retrieval system, or transmitted, in any form or by any means, electronic, mechanical, photocopying, recording, or otherwise, without the written permission of the author.

ISBN 978-1-934185-38-4

Published by Biblio Resource Publications, Inc.
108½ South Moore Street, Bessemer, MI 49911
info@biblioresource.com

A Read Aloud Curriculum Enrichment Product
www.RACEforHeaven.com

Cover art: Windows in the Cathedral of Our Lady of the Angels, Los Angeles, CA; originally created for St. Vibiana Cathedral, Los Angeles, by Franz Borgias Mayer

Scripture texts in this work are taken from the *New American Bible with Revised New Testament* © 1986, 1970 Confraternity of Christian Doctrine, Washington, D.C. and are used by permission of the copyright owner. All Rights Reserved. No part of the *New American Bible* may be reproduced in any form without permission in writing from the copyright owner.

Excerpts from the English translation of the *Catechism of the Catholic Church* for use in the United States of America Copyright 1994, United States Catholic Conference, Inc.— Libreria Editrice Vaticana. Used with Permission.

Excerpts from the English translation of the *Compendium of the Catechism of the Catholic Church* Copyright © 2005, Libreria Editrice Vaticana. All rights reserved. The exclusive licensee in the United States is the United States Catholic Conference of Catholic Bishops, Washington D.C., and all requests for United States uses of the *Compendium of the Catechism of the Catholic Church* should be directed to the United States Conference of Catholic Bishops.

Printed in the United States of America

Table of Contents

Introduction

THIS BOOK is intended to supplement a young Catholic's preparation for the Sacrament of Reconciliation by providing a basic doctrinal review of the sacrament as well as resources to assist in a thorough examination of conscience—a seven-day read-aloud formation retreat. Begin one week before the day of First Reconciliation, i.e., if Reconciliation day is a Saturday, begin the Saturday before. One possible format would be to read and discuss the lesson in the morning, the read-aloud stories in the afternoon, and work through the day's section of the examination of conscience in the evening. Continue this pattern each day, concluding the day before the sacrament is received.

Contained within this book are chapters pertinent to the Sacrament of Reconciliation from two Catholic books for children from the 1920's: *I Belong to God, Great Truths in Simple Stories for Children and Lovers of Children* by Lillian Clark; and *Children's Retreats in Preparation for First Confession, First Holy Communion, and Confirmation* by Rev. P.A. Halpin—the latter of which have provided the primary lessons for this book with Lillian Clark's material interspersed with other appropriate out-of-print Catholic material for children. Both of these primary sources carry the imprimatur of Patrick Cardinal Hayes of New York.

As with all RACE for Heaven products, the aim is to teach the tenets of the Roman Catholic Church in a read-aloud format that encourages families to *live* our Faith on a practical level. Therefore, the lessons have been supplemented with short stories and poems that provide insights in applying the doctrines of the Sacrament of Reconciliation to daily life. Several discussion points have been provided to promote the holy habit of spiritual conversation within your family—to encourage family members to speak holy thoughts—and to help you grow together in holiness. In addition, each lesson ends with an opportunity to pray about important aspects of the lesson and to learn new prayers.

The *Compendium of the Catechism of the Catholic Church* stresses (nos. 303 and 304) a careful examination of conscience as an essential element of the Sacrament of Reconciliation. Towards this end, an examination of conscience has been formulated according to the dictates of the *Catechism of the Catholic Church* (no. 1454). Each day of this retreat you are encouraged *as a family* to prayerfully read-aloud and consider each point of this examination as provided in the Appendix. As the retreat should, ideally, conclude with all members of the family participating in the Sacrament of Penance, please spend adequate time on this important section.

A Reconciliation Reader-Retreat is designed to not only prepare those making their first confession but also to enhance the experience of this sacrament for the entire family. Please attempt, as best as possible, to make these seven days truly a time of retreat. Allow time for recollection, quiet meditation, and Eucharistic adoration. Families may wish to read books or view movies on saints of interest. Cease as much as possible the frenzied activities of busy family life. Ask the Holy Spirit and your guardians angels for their intercession.

May our Risen Lord, who is present through His holy priests in the Sacrament of Penance, bless your family as you prepare to obtain His mercy and forgiveness in this sacrament.

Janet P. McKenzie
Feast of the Presentation of the Lord
February 2, 2011

Making a Retreat*

WHY AM I MAKING this little retreat?—to learn to know God and myself better.

Of course, every day I must try to know and serve and love God; that is really why I am in this world, but while I am making my retreat I am at the school of God—studying Him and studying myself very earnestly.

Often in my life I will be left alone with God, and so I should know Him very, very well and should like to be with Him—then we will be like two loving friends when we are left alone together. . . . When I was born, it was just God and me; in my prayers it is just God and I—in my confession, with my eyes closed, no one but God and I—in Holy Communion, with my head bowed low, I am alone with God—when life is ending and I am dying, all will be left behind, and then, too, it will be just God and I—and again after death, when I am standing before the great white throne, waiting to be sent to heaven or to hell, most surely, I will be alone with God my Creator, and my Father, and the great Lover of my soul.

So I really want to know Him very well. During these days I must try to think as little as I can about everybody and everything else and as much as I can of Him.

Making my meditation means kneeling at His knee, with play and people put out of my mind, reading quietly and very slowly, word by word, what is written here and thinking and praying quietly about it and about what it means.

May God the Father, God the Son, and God the Holy Spirit help me prepare to receive the Sacrament of Reconciliation worthily.

*From *I Belong to God, Great Truths in Simple Stories for Children and Lovers of Children* by Lillian Clark, Longmans, Green and Company, 1936.

Preparation Prayer*

Loving Father, through the intercession of the Sacred Heart of Jesus and the Immaculate Heart of Mary, please grant us the grace of listening attentively and understanding deeply the lessons of this retreat. We ask that you send the Holy Spirit down upon us so that we may be prepared, to the best of our abilities, to receive the mercy and forgiveness of our Lord Jesus Christ in the Sacrament of Penance and Reconciliation.

Through the intercession of our guardian angels, give us the grace to honestly examine our sins and failings in order to make a good confession. Strengthen us, Lord, and inspire us to work diligently so that our first [next] sacramental experience of Your mercy and forgiveness may be the perfect model for all future receptions of this sacrament. Please bless us with your abundant grace and help our family to grow in love for You and for each other as we participate together in this retreat. We ask this in the most precious name of our Friend and Savior, Jesus Christ.

Amen.

*Please pray this prayer together prior to each lesson of this retreat.

Lesson One
Introduction to the Sacrament of Confession

MY DEAR CHILDREN, in a few days you will go to the Sacrament of Penance and Reconciliation[1] for the first time. This sacrament must always be made well. So, in order that every time you confess your sins you may be sure that you have neglected nothing, and have told every one of your faults and have been sorry for them in the right way, the greatest care must be taken that the very first confession you make be so good that it will be the beginning of many, many confessions, all ending with the last, which will be at the hour of death, and will be so well done that you will not be afraid to die, but rather be glad. If this was not the case, we would not go to all the trouble to which you see we have gone to teach you how to perform this act as you should and as you must. You have been coming to catechism classes for several years. You may have had catechism lessons to learn by heart, and to learn in such a way that you will never forget them. You have probably been examined by your teachers and by your priest. Other children may have begun with you, but they are not receiving this sacrament with you, because either they did not learn their catechism well enough or they did not come regularly to their class.

---

[1] Although known formally as the Sacrament of Penance and Reconciliation, this sacrament is also (according to the *Catechism of the Catholic Church,* nos. 1423-1424) called the Sacrament of Confession, the Sacrament of Conversion, the Sacrament of Penance, the Sacrament of Forgiveness, and the Sacrament of Reconciliation. These terms are used interchangeably in this book.

1

You know well the part of your little book that must be learned before one can be allowed to approach the Sacrament of Penance. You have won a very great prize —the prize of being permitted to go to confession. It is a reward so great that it is only when you have entered heaven that you will know how great it is. You have not yet done all that is necessary; that is, you have not done enough to make yourselves ready for this wonderful sacrament. For the next seven days, we will meet and discuss the elements of this sacrament and you will work to examine your conscience quite thoroughly so that there will be nothing to prevent you from receiving this sacrament with sincere devotion and complete honesty with your sins and failings.

In the prayer we say at the beginning of each instruction[2], you will ask God, through the most Sacred Heart of Jesus and through the Immaculate Heart of Mary, to give you the grace of being attentive, of understanding, and of being made every minute more ready for the great day of your first confession. In this way I feel that, with God's help, you will be so happy after your first confession that you will always remember the day on which you made it, and will always be glad whenever the time comes for you to make other confessions. Pope Pius X, the great apostle of the early reception of the sacraments, wrote to all the bishops of the world begging of them to take care of all his little children, and to see that they were well prepared for all the sacraments, especially for those of Penance and Communion. Now, I ask you—since all that I say is true—I ask you, do you not think you should do your best to fit yourselves for the great sacrament? I hear every boy and every girl here

... we want the world to be good.

---

[2] See page iv of this book.

say "Yes "to my question. You know we want our children to be very good in every way. I think that you all want to be good, too. I am sure there is no one here that intends to be a bad girl or a bad boy, a bad man or a bad woman, is there? Why do we want you all to be good? Because we want the world to be good.

If everybody in the world was good, what a different world it would be! There would be no more cursing, nor swearing, nor stealing, nor becoming angry or jealous. Nobody would hurt another. There would be no more murder, and, perhaps, or rather certainly, no more wars. What a beautiful place this would be to live in then! Besides, then everybody would be saved, that is, everybody would go to heaven and be with God forever.

Now you see why we want all our children to be good, because then there is a chance that they will keep on growing good until they are men and women, and thus the world will be better for all that. Nothing helps more to make and keep children as they should be than going to confession. But if your confession is not made well, it will not help at all. It is pretty true that if your first confession is made properly, all your following confessions will be made properly, too. Now I have given you some reasons why you should do all you can to so prepare yourselves for this first confession that when it is over it will be something you will never forget and will always be glad to remember.

I am going to tell you about a remarkable CCD teacher. He is on the list of the holy ones of our Church; he is a saint. He is now in heaven. He has been there with God and Christ and the Blessed Virgin and the angels and the saints ever since he died, and that was over three hundred sixty years ago. That is a long while to be in heaven. So it may seem to you and me, but to him it has all passed like a flash. This saint's name is Joseph Calasanctius. He founded a society of priests. They were

3

called "The Poor Regular Clergy of the Pious Schools of the Mother of God." When he was a child and during his boyhood, he practiced all the virtues. At school he spoke very often of the wonderful things in the catechism, and especially about the best way of praying. He became a very learned man. He made a vow. Do you know what that means? It means a most solemn promise. He made a vow that he would be as good in thought, word and deed as it was possible for him to be. He was very fond of children, and they were very fond of him and liked to listen to him talking about confession and Communion and the other things of God. When he was but a child himself, he used to call them around him. He became a priest. He was a Spaniard, but went to Rome, and there did very many striking things for God and the Church. He was a lover of the poor, and during a plague he carried the bodies of the dead on his shoulders and buried them.

Finally, when the Holy Spirit spoke to him, he started a society of poor priests, and the duty of that society was to teach children. The poor children of that day did not have so many to teach them as you have now. That society went all over Europe gathering children together, teaching them the catechism and preparing them to receive the great sacraments of Penance and Communion.

This St. Joseph lived until he was ninety-one years old. The blessed Mother of God, to whom he was very dear—first, on account of his pure life, and, secondly, on account of the care he took of children— told him the day on which he was going to die, and on that day his sinless soul was received by her into heaven. This happened in the year sixteen hundred forty-eight. One hundred years after he left this world, his heart and tongue were found just as they had been in life.

Now I am sure you are asking me why I talk of this holy man. I know you are all asking what has this St.

Joseph to do with our catechism. The reason I spoke of him is this: If God loved him so much because he made teaching catechism the work of his life, I ask you, does that not show what God thinks of the need of children to know their catechism? Now what God thinks, my dear children, you must try and think, just as what God hates you must hate, and what God loves you must love.

You understand now that you should know your catechism better than anything else you know. In fact, you might know everything else—you might become very learned in all other things—but if you do not hold your catechism firmly in your memory, everything else will be worth nothing at all. You wonder why the priest speaks so very often about religion classes and the catechism. You see why now. You have learned in your religion classes and you have read in your catechism that God made you. Why did He make you? I see the answer on your lips. God made you. God was not obliged to make you—nobody could force Him to make you; He made you of His own free will. He must have made you for some reason. God never acts without a reason. You and I do sometimes, but the Lord—never.

God must have made you for some reason.

Your catechism tells you that He created you to know Him and to love Him and to serve Him in this life, and to be happy with Him forever in the next. If you do not know Him, or if you know Him and do not serve Him, you cannot be happy in the next world. If you are not happy in the other world, you are certainly going to be unhappy and miserable. And as the other world has no death in it—as in the next world everybody is going to live forever—it is as certain as certain can be, if one is unhappy there and wretched, one is unhappy and wretched forever and ever.

Not one of us wishes to be unhappy, even for a second, and surely not one of us could bear the thought of being unhappy forever. Children meet with all sorts of accidents about which we hear and read every day. They meet with terrible accidents; they lose their legs and their arms. They are crippled for life. Not only that, but they are killed. We cannot bear even to think of these things. Can you tell me which is worse: to be lame or blind, or deaf and dumb, or even to die, or, to go on living forever—forever, mind you, in the other world, without being cared for or loved by anybody, to be in darkness and in suffering more cruel than anything anybody has known in this life, and that always and without end? I know what your answer is. You will tell me at once that it is better—oh, better than anyone can think —to be in all kinds of pain here for years and years than to be in torture forever in the life after the grave.

It is your catechism which teaches you all this, and remember that in many parts of the world there are boys and girls who know nothing at all about these things. You would know nothing yourselves if there had not been your parents to tell you about it or to send you where you would hear about it. Suppose I ask you what you ought to do now that I have been telling you how necessary the catechism is; what will you answer? I think I hear you all say that, no matter how well you studied your religion lessons before, you are going to study harder now and until you make your first Communion and until you are confirmed, that is, until you receive the sacrament which gives you the Holy Spirit. I think I hear you all say that, no matter how careful you have been up to now in being present at every religion class, you will let nothing in the future keep you away.

Those are two good resolutions. "Resolution" is a big word, but I have an idea that you know what it means. When you make a resolution, you make a strong promise to God and to yourself that you will do something that pleases Him and is useful to you. Your catechism has taught you that it is more worth your while to be happy in the next world than to be happy here, that you must take more care of your soul than of your body, for the simple reason that the body will die one day and the soul will never die.

There is only one thing that can hurt the soul. What is that one thing? Sin. If, when you leave this world, there is a mortal sin on your soul, your soul will not die—because it cannot—but your soul will be in punishment always. You see at once that there is really only one thing to be afraid of, and that one thing is sin. There are very few who do not commit sin. Thank God there are a great many who never become guilty of mortal sin. But in case somebody does something that is so bad that we have to call it mortal sin, must that person keep that sin with him forever? Is there no way of getting rid of it? You will at once tell me that there is one sure way, and that one sure way is the Sacrament of Penance and Reconciliation. This sacrament, if it can take away sin from a man's soul, must be a wonderful thing, a most wonderful thing. Yet the Sacrament of Confession can do all that.

You are getting ready for that wonderful sacrament. Is it not clear to you that you cannot prepare yourselves too well? In these instructions, I am going to help you to be so ready the day you go to confession so that you will make no mistake, and do everything so well that when the priest tells you to leave the confessional, there will not be a single sin on your souls.

We are going to talk about confession and about confession only, and about everything that is a part of confession and about everything that has anything to do with confession—therefore about sacraments, examination of conscience, and above all about sin, so that you may learn to hate it more than anything in this life, so that you may learn to love with all your heart that great sacrament which has the power not only to wash away sin, but to make you so strong that you will be better able to resist sin.

Discussion Questions

1. How can one person, striving to be good—to become more like Jesus—make the world a better place? How does confession help us toward this goal?
2. Why is it important to prepare well for your first confession?
3. How can you imitate and honor St. Joseph Calasanctius?
4. What is your resolution as you begin this retreat?

I Talk with God

Kneel down and pray before a crucifix or an image of the Sacred Heart of Jesus, asking God to help you make a good confession, how to be heartily sorry for your sins, and how to keep your promise never again to sin. Then pray the "Miracle Prayer" of Fr. Peter Mary Rooker of the Servite Fathers:

Lord Jesus, I come before you just as I am. I am sorry for my sins. I repent of my sins, please forgive me. In your name I forgive all others for what they have done against me. I renounce Satan, the evil spirits and all their works. I give you my entire self, Lord Jesus, now and forever. I invite you into my life, Jesus. I accept you as my Lord, God and Savior. Heal me, change me, and strengthen me in body, soul and spirit.

Come, Lord Jesus, cover me with your Precious Blood, and fill me with your Holy Spirit. I Love You, Lord Jesus. I Thank You, Jesus. I shall follow you every day of my life. Amen.

Lesson One Read-aloud Story and Poem

This story, "God Creating, God Redeeming," is from *I Belong to God, Great Truths in Simple Stories for Children and Lovers of Children* by Lillian Clark, Longmans, Green and Company, 1936, pages 3-14.

T ODAY YOU ARE GOING to ask yourself a new question. Say once, twice, three times: "Do I belong to myself?" Ask it once more with your eyes closed: "Do I belong to myself?"

My! But that is strange! . . . "Do I belong to myself?" Yes, it is strange. It makes you feel like rubbing your eyes a bit; you want to look around cautiously, and you hope someone is near . . . and sure enough here am I— but let us see about it together.

Let us imagine that—

All night long the snow has been steadily falling and covering everything with "a silence deep and white," and today is a holiday—how glorious! You dress in a flash; your breakfast is hardly more than a pause on your way to the door—and out you go into the yard. "I say, this is great," you cry, "packs fine." Then an idea comes into your mind.

You work away quickly and noiselessly. Balls are rolled, balls are shaped, and at the end of a happy morning you are not alone in the yard. I see standing beside you a portly figure in white—a motionless, silent man is reflecting your pleasure in a broad, merry, and unchanging smile. Snowbirds stop their rapid flights, and resting on a branch of a nearby tree, admire your work. You do look pleased, and you have certainly made a splendid snowman. Presently, you are joined by your friends and I hear you say, "Isn't he great!" And then—

"Say, look out, he's mine. . . . Look what you're doing; he belongs to me. I made him."

You have grown fond of him as you worked over him, and you are quite right—yes—quite, quite right in saying, "He is mine," because the work of your hands is your own and you can honestly say, "I made him; he belongs to me."

[Keep "I made him—he belongs to me—he is mine" in the back of your mind for a time, and we shall consider another picture.]

This morning—

On your way to school, you bought a new ball. It is springtime, and the air is thrilling with the twittering of the birds, and the lightness of your heart is in accord with the gladness of the morning. Of course, the ball is to remain out of sight until after school. You work earnestly, trying not to hear the distracting chirpings coming in through the open windows—trying hard, too, to stay put at your books for the year-end exams are coming. You keep at it even though you get the scent of apple and peach blossoms, and can almost hear the new grass growing and the gentle swaying of the ripening grains.

At last the day is finished, and the lines are forming for dismissal. Blessed three o'clock! "Is there any hour quite like three o'clock?" you are thinking when you are roused by the teacher's voice. "Who owns this ball? It was found in the aisle."

"Oh," you say, darting forward, "that is mine. I bought it this morning." Of course, it is given back to you at once for it is quite true that what you buy belongs to you.

[Keep also in your mind—"What I buy belongs to me. It is mine."]

And now again—

It is a balmy autumn day, and the dog your father gave you for your birthday is romping on the lawn in the long shadows of the late afternoon sun. A friend comes to visit you, and you say, "Oh, come along, you must see my new dog."

"Rex, Rex," you call. "Is he not a beauty?" He comes to you with a bound and as you stroke his tan coat you say, "He's mine, all mine. Is he not a great birthday gift?"

[Keep this too: "What is given to me belongs to me. It is mine."]

Now let us get back to our question. Can you say really and honestly, "I belong to myself"? Be fair.

"W-e-l-l, I belong to myself if I can say I made myself, I bought myself, I gave me myself."

Yes, can you say it? Can a person make himself? Men can make wonderful things—pictures that move and rockets that fly to the moon, but can a man make himself? . . . No, no man can make anything that has life in it, not even a blade of grass.

Can a person buy himself, or can a person be the gift of anyone on this earth? . . . No, these things are impossible. Then you did not make yourself, nor buy yourself nor were you your own gift. So you do not belong to yourself, nor do you belong to anyone in this world.

"Who then owns me, do I belong to no one, am I a lost child?" No, there is Someone to whom you belong and not only in one of these ways but in all three, and that Someone is the great GOD. Yes, this is so, and it is very, very wonderful. . . . The work of His Hands is surely His. . . . You had snow to start with, but He has made everything and everybody in the wide, wide world out of nothing—even you and me.

Have you never seen men in large cities flying along high above your head on a cloudless day writing signs across the blue sky in fluffy, white rope-letters that you easily read from the ground? How fitting if they should write in the heavens: I BELONG TO GOD . . . and not only there but swing these popcorn rope-letters over trees and lands and seas and fields— across everything in this marvelous world—having everything proudly repeating these blessed words—"I belong to God."

"Did God make Himself, too?" Ah no, He was never made. Do you not remember the catechism says, "God had no beginning—He always was and always will be"?

Jane will help us here—

She had come to the church with her brothers, Jack and Jesse, to stay for a three-day retreat for First Communion. They were earnestly trying to prepare themselves for the great day when our Lord would come into their hearts for the first time, and they had had many periods of silence in the chapel to think over what they would say to the dear God when He was really the Guest of their hearts.

Finally, the evening before the eventful day had arrived, and all was ready. Quite angel-like—snow-white souls and yearning hearts—they were seated quietly on the lawn for a last talk before bedtime when Sister asked, "Jane, what are you going to say to our Lord when He comes tomorrow?"

Jane moved out to the edge of the garden seat, as she always did when she had something important to say, and sitting up straight and tall, she began: "I am going to ask Him"—her clear voice quivered slightly with emotion, but she did not hesitate a second—"I'm going to

ask Him where He was when He had that first beginning. . . ."

Sister, as well as the boys, felt it was an awe-inspir-
ing moment. Jane was just six, and the child's soul was
in her eyes, where a little mist of pain had gathered,
her earnestness was so intense.

Sister was the first to speak. "Do you remember what
the catechism says about that, Jane?" (That lesson had
been studied six months ago but Jane had a splendid
memory.)

"Yes," quickly, "but He must have had a beginning—
everything has."

"In His human nature, yes," Sister softly replied. "He
had His beginning in His human nature on that blessed day when the angel Gabriel announced to the little
Virgin Mary that she could be the dear Mother of God,
and then came the wonderful moment at last, when, as
every other little one, the Infant-God was lying in the
arms of His blessed Mother—you have seen Him, dear,
in the stable of Bethlehem—the lovely, wee, Babe—our
precious, tiny Baby-Brother.

"But Jane," Sister continued, "In His divine nature,
he never had a beginning—never, no—never. It is one
of God's privileges, and we do believe it. We cannot easily understand it—but it is true—God had no beginning."

"Then . . . then," said Jane, "I shall ask Him to tell
me, please, how it could be"—this with a weary little
sigh . . . a sigh in which the awful torment of days, perhaps months, seemed to escape. Jane is a philosopher.

But we have wandered—

Besides making you, God bought you from the dreadful slavery of Satan by paying for you with the Precious
Blood of His own beloved Son. And still more, on the

day when you were baptized, you were given to Him by the words spoken by your godfather and godmother . . . you are His Gift. . . . That day He reached out eagerly and lovingly to receive you, and He folded you closely to His Heart as soon as the cleansing waters of Baptism made your soul beautiful, and pure, and radiant with grace. Right then, God became your very own Father and you His little child. How very, very wonderful!

Do I belong to myself? . . . Goodness, no. I should say not.

I belong to God. He made me. He bought me. I am His gift—His little child.

Oh, my God, I believe I came from You and I am going back to You fast. . . . While I was a baby, I could not understand these mighty truths, but I am a baby no longer.

Now let us see what it means to belong to God.

Well . . . if your snowman could move or walk, or could work and think and love, you would, of course, expect him to stay near you and work with you and help you. And you would expect him to love you and I am sure he would, for he would not be a snowman but for you.

Oh, my Father, I understand. I can move and walk and work and think and love, and I must be very glad to do all these things for the God who made and owns me. Almighty God, You have a three-times right to expect me to please you—to know You, to love You, to serve you . . . this is why I am here: To know and love and serve You, Lord, and Your Will alone to do—then safely to rest, Father, in Your hands, knowing I belong to You.

Oh, my God, how sweet it is to know I belong to You.

14

If I belonged to anyone on this earth, someday I should be left alone, but You will always be in Your lovely home up there guarding me, and guiding me, and waiting for me. Your loving Heart is ever the same yesterday, today and forevermore. Help me each day, my dearest Father, to be your good child—knowing You better, loving You better, serving and pleasing You always better.

(Now, happy child of God, close your eyes, and speak to Him as simply as you do to your mother or to your little friends. Speak to Him very lovingly, and very sweetly, and very earnestly, and thank Him again and again for the grace of belonging to Him. Say everything that is in your heart and at the end, say the Our Father.)

———

The following poem is written by Sr. M. Josita and is from her book, *Sing a Song of Holy Things,* Tower Press, 1945, page 50.

"God's Help"

God is very near each day,
So when I work or when I play
I say, "My Jesus, help!"

Just as soon as I awake,
And promise things for His dear sake,
I add, "My Jesus, help!"

Whenever hard things come my way,
I always stop and quickly say,
"My Lord, my Jesus, help!"

Jesus hears me when I call;
He gives His helping grace to all
Who say, "My Jesus, help!"

———

Discussion Questions

1. For three reasons, we belong to God. In what way has God made us? How has He bought us? How have we been given to Him?

2. We do not always act or think as children of God— as children who belong to God. Describe several actions or ways of thinking that illustrate this. Why is it important to always act and think as someone who belongs to God?

3. What does it mean to belong to God? What are the rewards? What is the cost?

4. Why is it important to ask Jesus to help us throughout each day?

Prayerfully read through Section I of "A Gospel Examination of Conscience" beginning with the introduction on page 146. End this examination session by praying an Act of Contrition or a prayer of your own creation.

Lesson Two
The Sacrament

MY DEAR CHILDREN, the first thing you have to know about confession is that it is a word that tells only of one part of the great sacrament for which you are trying to make yourselves ready and worthy. Confession means: making something known to someone besides ourselves. For you just now, to confess is to make known your sins to a priest. Still, that is not the whole sacrament. The sacrament is whole when, after you have told your sins to the priest, you show your sorrow and receive from him some penance and then absolution. Yet though we use the word "confession," which is only a part of the sacrament, we mean the entire sacrament.[3] To understand what confession is, then, you must fix in your minds what a sacrament is, what confession is, what absolution is, and what penance or satisfaction is.

Everything must be clear in your thoughts about what you learn in your catechism, but above all the words of the catechism must be held without any change by you. When asked a question, the words you use in answering must be those of your little book. Never change them. You may not know just now all that they mean, but later you will, and you will find in them a great help to let others know what your Holy Church teaches.

I am going to talk about the Sacrament of Penance. So we will run over the words of our catechism to find out first what a sacrament is, and secondly, what the Sacrament of Confession is.

---

[3] For this reason, the term "Sacrament of Penance and Reconciliation" is now the preferred title of this sacrament.

What is a sacrament? Before I begin to explain what a sacrament is, I will tell you a little bit of history about the catechism. Your catechism is a very small book. More than four hundred sixty years ago, at a place called Trent, which is a town in Austria, the pope called together the bishops and doctors of the Church. At his bidding in that far-off place came together many archbishops and bishops and some sixty priests. They were from nearly everywhere. This great meeting was more than once obliged to give up its work, sometimes on account of the plague, sometimes on account of wars, again on account of the death of a pope. Altogether, with breaks, it lasted from 1545 until 1563—that is eighteen years. During all their meetings, they spoke of many things concerning the Catholic Church, but there is one thing they had always before their minds, and that one thing was the catechism. These archbishops and bishops ordered that a catechism should be made, that it should be printed in all the languages of the world and explained to the people. It was a very large book when finished, but in your little catechism you have, taken out of that large book, everything that is necessary for you to know in order to be a Catholic who understands what he believes, as well as to be a Catholic who thinks and speaks and acts as a true, that is, as a real Catholic should.[4]

> In your catechism you have . . . everything that is necessary for you to know.

---

[4] The *Catechism of the Council of Trent* (the *Roman Catechism*) was intended for priests; later, the *Baltimore Catechism* was developed in the United States as a shorter, teaching catechism. In 1992, Pope John Paul II authorized the publication of the *Catechism of the Catholic Church* as an "authentic reference text for teaching Catholic doctrine and particularly for preparing local catechisms" (*Fidei Depositum*).

You see how much the Church thinks of the catechism and how much you should love your little book, which means so much for you now and will always mean much for you. That catechism, of which I have just told you the history, answers the question which I asked above.

You remember that question was: What is a sacrament? A sacrament, says the catechism of Trent, is a visible sign of invisible grace instituted by Christ for our justification. Your little book may use different words, but they mean the same thing. Your catechism calls a sacrament an outward sign of inward grace, instituted by Christ to give grace to our souls. The words we use to tell what a thing is are called a definition. I have given you the definition of a sacrament, and in order to understand the definition, we must take every word of it and get at the meaning of each one.

There is the word which will be used very often these days; it is the word *sacrament*. Sacrament, in a general way, means something holy. Everything is holy that has to do with God, with Christ, with the saints, with the Church. You know what holy water is. It is blessed by the priest for those who belong to the Church, and it cannot be used in the same way as other water is used. The chalice and all the

> A sacrament is an outward sign, instituted by Christ, to give grace.

vessels belonging to the Church are holy. They cannot be used as other vessels are made use of. Even the church is holy. You may not act in it as you would in your own houses. A holy thing is something that must be treated differently from all other things.

You remember, perhaps, hearing that when Moses was keeping the sheep of his master, he came to a mountain, and looking up he saw a figure in a flame of fire, and in the midst of a bush. The bush was on fire but

19

was not burned. As he was going near he heard a voice saying: "Come no nearer! Remove the sandals from your feet, for the place where you stand is holy ground.[5]" Because it was holy, he could not walk on that ground as he would on other ground. All this shows how careful we must be about holy things. Now, what you must always keep in mind is that a sacrament, that every sacrament, is holy, and therefore you would be doing wrong to behave toward it as you behave toward other things.

This much learned, we will study with care every word in that little phrase which defines, that is which tells you, what a sacrament is. There are three things necessary to make up a sacrament. These three things are (a) an outward sign, (b) founded by Christ, (c) to give us grace; that is, to make us holy. When you have all these three, you have a sacrament. If even one of these three things is missing, you have no sacrament. I have, therefore, to teach what an outward sign is, what we mean when we say "instituted by Christ," and what "giving grace" is. After all that is made clear, I will show how these three things are found in confession or in penance.

What is an outward sign? It is a sign which can be seen, which is not hidden. I suppose you all can tell me what a sign is. You use signs very often. Sometimes in school, a boy or girl puts up a hand. That is a sign for the teacher. Let me tell you right here that a sign is something that lets us know something else. To come back to my example: A hand is raised in class. No word is said to the teacher, but still the teacher knows not only that you have lifted up your hand, but that either you wish to answer something which he has asked, or that you

> A sign is something that lets us know something else.

---

[5] Exodus 3:5

want to get some permission. That lifting up of your hand is an outward sign, because it can be seen. You are going along the street and in a window you see a little dress; that dress is a sign that in the store to which the window belongs they sell dresses for little girls. These are all signs. If you see tears in your mother's eyes, those tears are a sign that your mother is suffering or is weeping for some loss—so much for signs.

Now, a sacrament must be a sign which tells you of something else, of something more than you can see, of something that is being done, of something that is going on. What takes place or what is being done, or what is going on in confession? You are being forgiven your sins; God is pardoning you everything that you have done against Him. What outward sign have we of all that? What is there in the Sacrament of Reconciliation which makes us know that sins are being forgiven? What do you see? You see a kneeling child in presence of a priest. There, you say at once, is a poor child making a confession of all his faults to the priest, who takes the place of God. You say that child would not do that if he did not expect to be forgiven. All that you see in the Sacrament of Penance is an outward sign of all that God does for those who go to confession. Penance, therefore, is an outward sign, and in so much begins to be a sacrament.

The second of those three things without which you cannot have a sacrament is that every sacrament must be instituted by Christ; that is, must be made by Christ. The Church cannot make a sacrament, nor the pope, nor a cardinal, nor a bishop, nor a priest, nor anyone but Christ. I will try to explain to you why this is so. What do the seven sacraments give to everyone who receives them in the right way? I hear you all say the seven sacraments give grace. But grace is very hard to understand. It will be enough for me just now to tell you that grace is a gift of God. It is called a gift of God because nobody but God can give it. Now, as every sacrament holds grace within itself, as there is no sacrament without grace, you may readily understand that only God, or Christ—who is both God and man—can make a sacrament. For since there is in every sacrament grace—since the sacrament is meant for no other end than to give grace—every sacrament must be made by God, or Christ, who is the only one who can give grace.

So, how do we know that Christ made this sacrament? We know it because the Church tells us, and whatever the Church teaches God teaches, who can neither deceive me nor be deceived by me. Besides, if you take up your New Testament some day and turn to the sixteenth chapter of St. Matthew, you will read that our Lord said to St. Peter, ". . . you are Peter, and upon this rock I will build my church, and the gates of the netherworld shall not prevail against it. I will give you the keys to the kingdom of heaven. Whatever you bind on earth shall be bound in heaven; and whatever you loose on earth shall be loosed in heaven."[6]

> Only God, or Christ, can make a sacrament.

In saying these words He gave, through St. Peter, the first head of the Church after Christ, to all the priests that have been in the world and will be in the world until the end of time, the power to forgive sins: in other words He, that is Christ, instituted the Sacrament of Penance in which sins are pardoned.

We have now put two parts of the sacrament together. There remains for us to look at the third part. Not only must a sacrament be an outward sign and be instituted by Christ, it must also give grace. I wonder if it be possible for me to make you understand what grace

---

[6] Matthew 16:18-19

is? In the first place, it is something from God, and from God alone. Moreover, it is something invisible—something which does not fall under our eyes or under any of our five senses. Again, it is something real, something real like the stars—like electricity, like air, like a perfume. We know that there are things which our eyes have never seen, and yet we are certain they are really something. You have never seen the breeze, but you know it really has being; it is a real something. Grace, too, though you have never looked at it or felt it in any way, is a real thing. It is something which God alone can give, it is invisible, it is real, and, lastly, it is strength.

I may use the word definition as much as I wish now, because I told you the meaning of it. The definition of grace would be something like this: Grace is a gift of God that helps us to be good in thought, in word, and in deed; which helps us to keep all His commandments. It is a free gift. God is not obliged to give us grace, but He will give it to us whenever we ask for it in the right way, and whenever we do what He tells us we must do in order to get it. It is not only a free gift, it is necessary for us. Without it, we cannot even pronounce as we should the holy name of Jesus. Without it, we cannot avoid sin; without it, we cannot live well, we cannot die well, we cannot be saved, we cannot enter the Kingdom of Heaven. In the Sacrament of Penance, we receive many graces; so many, in fact, that we cannot count them.

> Grace is a gift of God; it is strength.

This preparation you are making for your first confession is a grace, the wish you all have to make a good confession is a grace; the sorrow you are beginning to feel for your sins even now is a grace; your telling every one of your faults without hiding a single one of them is a grace. But all these graces are not the great grace of confession. The chief grace of the Sacrament of Penance is being made clean in your souls, in your words, in your thoughts, in your actions; the great grace—the special grace of confession—is being pardoned your sins, is being made holy, is being made just. Sin makes the soul ugly. Sin soils, sin spots the soul. The grace of the sacrament, which in a few days you are going to receive for the first time, will whiten your souls and take away all the spots.

Is not grace, which does all this, a sweet and a lovely and a beautiful angel of God? You know what money is and what it can do. Yet not all the money in the world can do for you what grace can. Yet, grace is a kind of money more precious than any gold. It can buy bright thoughts and pure words and deeds worth more than pearls for you.

My dear children, I want one thought to be on your minds every minute of every hour of every one of these last days of preparation. It is the thought that in your first confession God is going to dress your souls in the beautiful robe of His grace. Beg of Him to help you to keep that robe as beautiful as it is when He puts it on you when you make your first confession—to keep it beautiful always, so that when you lie down in death there will not be a stain upon it, there will not be a tear in it, but it will still be a garment rich and lovely enough to pass through the doors of heaven with and to be glad with among the angels forever and forever.

––––––––

Discussion Questions

1. What are the three parts of the Sacrament of Penance and Reconciliation? Referring to page 145 of

this book, discuss the five elements necessary to receive this sacrament worthily.

2. What are the three things necessary to make a sacrament?
3. What is the outward sign of the Sacrament of Confession?
4. For what reason is every sacrament made?
5. What is the definition of grace? Tell what grace is in your own words. Why is grace important?
6. Describe clearly what your garment of grace looks like. If you like, you may draw the beautiful robe of grace in which God clothes you when you make a good confession.

I Talk with God

Meditate on the following passage from Rev. A. M. Grussi's *The Little Follower of Jesus (A Book for the Young Folks Based and Built on the "The Following of Christ" by Thomas à Kempis)*, P. J. Kenedy, 1892, pages 191-192:

> Thomas à Kempis says: "This is the reason why the gifts of grace cannot flow in us, because we are ungrateful to the Giver, nor do we return all to the Fountainhead.
>
> So it is. God has done so much for us. He continues always to offer us new graces. But instead of thanking Him for the graces He offers us, we frequently disregard them, or even refuse to receive them. Therefore, God withholds many a grace from us that He would otherwise bestow upon us for our further sanctification; and He give it to others, more willing than we are, who receive it with gratitude, and make good use of it. . . .

Yes, my dear children, let us ever be thankful to God for the graces He gives us. Whether the hand of Jesus strokes us consolingly, or whether it strikes us with tribulation, let us kiss it in humble gratitude; for, says *The Following [Imitation] of Christ*: "He that desires to retain the grace of God, let him be thankful for grace when it is given, and patient when it is withdrawn. Let him pray that it may return; let him be cautious and humble, lest he lose it."

Pray Sister M. Imelda's prayer asking the Holy Spirit to pour His grace upon you:

Come, Holy Spirit. Come into my mind. Come, Holy Spirit. Come into my heart. You can give me the strength and the courage to confess my sins even though I may be afraid. Give me the grace to know my sins. Give me the grace to confess them honestly and without fear. Holy Spirit, help me make a good confession. Give me strength to be brave in the future. Amen.

For older children and adults: Acknowledging that we belong to God, He made us, and all we have is His, we pray St. Ignatius' prayer of self-dedication:

Lord Jesus Christ, take all my freedom, my memory, my understanding, and my will. All that I have and cherish You have given me. I surrender it all to be guided by your will. Your grace and your love are wealth enough for me. Give me these, Lord Jesus, and I ask for nothing more. Amen.

Lesson Two Read-aloud Stories and Poem

This story is from *I Belong to God, Great Truths in Simple Stories for Children and Lovers of Children* by Lillian Clark, Longmans, Green and Company, 1936, pages 55-66.

"Misers or Fireflies–Which?"
(Going to Heaven by Grace)

GOING TO HEAVEN by grace . . . this is just lovely. I am glad that today I am to think about heaven. I have chosen heaven and I have made up my mind that it is to be my home when my life here is ended. I simply love to think of it. I love to imagine that I can hear the angels' laughter and their blissful songs, and I do want to find out the surest, safest way to reach it.

Going to heaven by grace!

Tell me, sweetest Jesus, what is grace? If it is grace that is to draw me to You, can I not begin this very day to get it? Please help me to know about it, and each day to have more and more.

But now, let us go back in our thoughts to the time before the dear Son of God had come to earth to be the sweet little Lord Jesus of Bethlehem. That was long, long ago, even thousands of years.

In those days, God the Father from His heavenly home was looking down with pity on our poor earth, and longing to send His beloved Son to save it from rushing madly on in sin to hell. But, His Son must have a mother, and who of all people was holy and pure and lovely enough for that? No one yet. But God, infinite and almighty, knows that such a mother will one day be upon this earth—a fit and ready soul—the Virgin Immaculate.

From His heavenly home the earth is spread out before the Eternal Father as the vast, deep, open sky is above us when we stand on a high hill at twilight's hush, seeing nothing above us but the soft, pretty, glimmering stars resting in its dark, deep blue. And our earth (God's sky—did you ever think of that?) is sparkling and dancing with stars for Him too. Can you guess what these stars are? (Not real ones, of course, but I think you can understand what I mean.) Oh! It is so sweet—they are the souls of His own dear creatures. "But do souls shine?"

Yes—that is, they have their *spiritual shinings*. Once, you know, when our Lord was on earth they said, "His face shone like the sun[7]." In this way, we can speak of souls shining. "But what makes them do it?" Read on a few moments longer, and you shall know.

Let us go back in imagination to the centuries before our Savior was born and let us watch the tender glance of the almighty Father, as it travels lovingly from soul to soul, as a bee from blossom to blossom, ever waiting and waiting. He sees some souls as wee baby stars, faintly twinkling and blinking; others as larger ones and others larger still with a brighter, clearer light. Then sometimes God finds a soul so very, very beautiful—glowing so ardently—but not yet, not yet; none perfect enough yet to be the holy mother.

But—sweetness and hope! At last one year just when summer is melting away in the blue haze of autumn, and the mellow sun and the harvest moon take turns in caressing the fruit-laden earth, the all-patient Father sees in the rich, quiet green of a rolling country, far, far from the noisy city, in the little village of Naza-

---

[7] Matthew 17:2

reth, a new soul—as a tiny star—shine suddenly forth. Watch Him as He bends lovingly over it—the silence of the world of grace veiling the scene.

In most ways this is much like other souls—other stars—but in two ways it is different. Shall I tell you how? Well, first, it delights to cover its lovely light from all but God and just to nestle like a shy, whispering violet at His feet, in all its peaceful beauty—shining only for Him; and besides, from the very beginning, it appeared each hour greater and lovelier. (All souls, you know, do not do this.)

Not many months had passed till it was much more beautiful than souls much older, and the most wonderful thing about it was, that it was never at a standstill. Never—no never—a ray less dim, but ever growing deeper—softer—clearer. What pleasure God took in gazing down upon it; how it held His most tender looks, and how its beauty caught the glances of all His fair angels! That little nook where it rested was the dearest place on earth to God, and that soul was its dearest treasure. It was His most precious pearl, glorious in His sight. . . . The angels wondered. . . . They loved the moon-kissed beauty of the midnight dew, they loved the joyous morning air when roses unfold and laughter fills the land, but never had they seen created beauty such as this—never before had they seen on earth so heavenly a soul.

"Could even an angel be more pure?" they said. "What does it mean?" God soon answered them. He gathered them about Him and told them the great secret. The long-awaited soul had come; the perfect soul; the soul holier than angels even—the soul fit to be God's mother.

They listened in a hush of ecstasy—and her name? Can you not tell it?—The little Virgin Mary.

Time passed, and then calling to His side the great angel Gabriel, God sent him with a wonderful message: "Would she like to be the mother of His Son?" What a glorious invitation! Softly and swiftly through the star-lit night he sped, and when Gabriel reached her little room, his greeting was, "Hail, Full of Grace."

Now you know—you know what makes souls shine and glow. The angel Gabriel has told the secret. "Full of Grace," he said—grace, blessed grace—grace is God's image in the soul—the flame of divine love burns there. Yes, it is grace that sets loving souls aglow, and we like to think of them scattered all through God's sky shining as the stars.

So grace is a very important thing, is it not? How God must love it! It was really grace that drew His divine Son from His bosom and brought Him to Mary to be our dear Savior.

"Oh, it must be truly beautiful," you say. "Could I not see some, just once, just for a moment?" No, no one here can see it. The little playmates of the little Mary, nor even her holy mother, Saint Ann, ever caught one glimpse of that glorious light blazing within her. It needs the eyes we are to have one day in heaven to see grace— this wondrous grace—but it is very real, even so.

Did you never think that there are many very real things on this earth that we have never heard nor seen? That somehow since our mother Eve's sin, our ears and eyes have never been just right? They are slow and dull. So, we miss many lovely things. We miss the soft, low sound of the grass as it grows; we miss the glad notes of the flowers as their petals uncurl; we miss the gentle words the summer breezes whisper. We cannot see the air all around us, yet so real and so important is it that not even for a moment could we live without it. And just so is it with grace (though we do not see it). The instant our soul loses it, it loses its precious life. So there can be no doubt, you simply must have grace. For no grace—no heaven.

Gracious me! What can I do about it? Do this—begin today to be a very miser of grace. Do you know what a miser is? He is the man you read about in story books. The man who somehow gets a bit of money and loves it so, that he takes it out at night when the doors are closed; when all is still; when other eyes are shut, and he looks it up and down and round about and hugs it to his heart, and then when morning dawns, back to its hiding place it goes and off goes Mr. Miser to work to earn a little more. His food he begs, for never a penny will he spend, and night after night, coin after coin, he drops into his treasure bag. How his eyes shine, how his smile spreads as he sees his gleaming pile grow higher and rounder!

Now just such a miser, you must be. Yes, a miser of grace. At Baptism, God gave you a precious grace to start with, and now it is for you to be off like the miser, winning more and more. And goodness me, how easy it is! Not hard work like the miser's. Simply a Sign of the Cross, well made, an Our Father, a Hail Mary; a true confession, a loving Communion, and Holy Mass (these bring enormous graces), yes, even to whisper with love the sweet names of Jesus and Mary.

This is your way of working for grace. Is it not pleasant?

Why, you can start right away with the first sleepy stir in the morning, blessing yourself as you waken, and you need not stop until you are back again in your bed at night and you fall off into the Land of Nod. And it can be your own little secret with God, no one around you need know of the wonderful treasures you gather, for none can see your gleaming, glowing graces—none but your dear guardian angel who kneels by your side, with eyes of ecstasy, as he sees God's own beauty growing in you.

And, of course, like a good miser, not even a cent will you waste. "How do I waste grace?" Why, by sinning. That's how. One big sin costs the whole pile—think of it. Then, alas! What a soul! And what trouble to start in again!

Did you never try on a summer's evening to follow a firefly, and was it not so hard that at last you gave it up? Hither and thither you go, and the light goes too, doesn't it, and you lose your firefly just when you think you have found it? It never grows any stronger. It never gets any brighter, but merely flashes in and out . . . in and out . . . and at last it goes out for good—and Mr. Firefly dies.

So it is with us and our precious grace if we are careless about saving it—if we spend it in sinning. Friday, perhaps, we do some wicked thing, and, ah me! Out goes the light. Saturday we are sorry and make a good confession, and lo! Our soul glows with God's grace, and is dear to Him again. But the next day a new sin, and darkness once more. And so it is. Some people spend their lives that way. Their store of grace never grows higher; its light never shines brighter; but it is in and out, in and out, all the time, their whole lives long.

Dear me! What if my light should be out when the angel of death comes to take me from this world! Mercy me! No grace, no heaven!

Dear God, sweet Lord, loving Father, does my soul please You? Can You see it glowing? Does it shine at all? Oh, I thank you that there is such a thing as grace. I thank You that there is something that can make my soul dear to Your heart, something that can draw Your tender looks toward it.

How good You were, O my Father, to make my soul precious in Your sight when I was a little baby, at my baptism, even before I knew anything about grace. Dear Father, forgive me if I have ever grieved You, by losing Your gift, by letting grace slip away in sin, by letting my soul grow cold and dark. Help me, sweetest Savior, to do better now; help me to be a real, real miser; help me to grow daily in grace; help me that each day my soul may glow more and more, until it blazes so brightly and burns so deeply with grace and love, that You will take me at last, to rest forever in Your loving arms.

[Close your eyes, little miser of grace, and be very quiet and tell our Lord in your own words just how you are going to try to win more grace. Then pray out loud the Our Father.]

From Book 41 in the serial, *Catholic Children's Treasure Box*, by the Maryknoll Sisters, 1960, the following story is entitled, "Jesus Forgives Our Sins," pages 1282-1297.

THIS STORY begins one day when Jesus was sitting on top of a mountain. He was looking across at the city of Jerusalem. And Jesus was sad.

Jesus was thinking about all of the people who lived

in the world at different times and in different places. He was thinking about you and me. And Jesus was sad because people wouldn't listen to Him. Even now, lots of people won't let Him help them. And Jesus loves them all so very much.

Here on the mountain, close beside Jesus, was a hen with her little chicks under her wings. Jesus said, "I want to gather all those people up in My arms and keep them safe, just as the hen gathers up her little chicks."

Jesus talked to the people of Jerusalem. He said, "Come to Me. I will forgive your sins and help you be good." But the people in Jerusalem wouldn't listen to Him. They kept on being wicked, and would not be sorry for their sins. We, too, say we want to be good. Then we fight, or tell a lie, or say, "I won't!" to our parents. But Jesus knows when we are sorry, and He loves us all very much. He wants to help us. . . .

On Easter Sunday night, Jesus came to visit His apostles. He said to them, "Peace be to you!" That meant: "Don't be afraid. I am Jesus." Jesus knew there would always be lots of people with sins on their souls who would want to get their sins forgiven. So He said to the apostles: "When you forgive sins, they are forgiven." Jesus was taking care of things so we could get our sins forgiven, after He went back to heaven. How wonderful!

Jesus works through the priest in the confessional. When the priest sits there, to forgive your sins, Jesus uses the priest's ears to listen. Jesus uses the priest's lips to say the words: "I absolve you." That means, "I wash away your sins." Jesus uses the priest's hand to bless you.

The first Easter Sunday was the day Jesus gave us the Sacrament of Penance. Lots of people don't know He did that. How happy they would be, if they knew, and could get their sins forgiven.

How kind Jesus is to us! Now anybody can have his sins wiped away by being sorry and telling them to the priest in confession. This is what we call the Sacrament of Penance. Only God can forgive sins, and Jesus is God. God uses the priest to forgive our sins. When we go to confession and tell our sins as best we can, we give our sins to Jesus. Jesus made up for our sins on the Cross. God gives us special grace in the Sacrament of Penance to make us very strong and good.

"St. Jerome" is taken from *Catechism in Stories, Revised Edition*, 1956, by Rev. Lawrence G. Lovasik, page 256.

ST. JEROME in his younger days had seen and enjoyed the pleasures of the world, for he was attached to a royal court. In his old age, he went to Palestine to do penance for his sins. Praying, fasting, and translating the Holy Bible into Latin, he spent his time in a desert near Bethlehem.

One day a beautiful little boy appeared to him and held out his arms as if he wanted something. His eyes seemed to be filled with tears, pleading for some favor. Jerome knew it was Jesus as soon as the boy began to speak.

"Now that you have come back, Jerome, what are you going to give me?"

"Jesus, I'll give you my heart and my love."

But the child seemed to want something more, and yet did not speak a word.

"I'll give you my work," said Jerome. "I'll give you my penances. What else can I give you, my Lord?"

And Jesus replied, "Jerome, give me your sins, that I may wash them away!"

Application: Jesus wanted Jerome to confess his sins often and to humble himself for having committed them. In this way he would show his gratitude for the graces in this sacrament. It is good to humble yourself for all the sins you have committed in your past life even if you have confessed them before. You may mention them in a general way at each confession, but at least be sorry for them before each confession. Imitate St. Jerome in his life of penance not only by doing your penance after confession, but also by coming to confession often so that you may let Jesus take your sins away, because they make you displeasing to Him.

The following story, "The Penny Man" is a story from Rev. Gerald T. Brennan's book, *Angel Food for Jack and Jill*, The Bruce Publishing Company, 1950, pages 46-49.

DURING THE PAST TWENTY YEARS, a Cleveland man has been a happy miser. During all that time this man has never spent a cent. That's right! During the past twenty years, this Cleveland man has never spent a penny.

Most misers, you know, are very unhappy. They think only about money—how they can make more money—how they can save more money. Then, too, misers are always worrying about their money because they are afraid they are going to lose it. That's why most misers are unhappy. But this Cleveland man is a different kind of miser. He's a happy miser, and he never spends a cent.

This man saves every penny he gets. When he goes to the store, when he buys gas, when he goes to the movies, he never spends the pennies he receives in change. He saves them. Of course, the man spends nickels and dimes and quarters and dollar bills. He buys whatever he needs, but he never uses pennies. What does the man do with his pennies?

Well, this man has a large iron bank and he puts every penny he gets into the bank. Now, the man doesn't save those pennies for himself. Oh, no! The man saves the pennies for some of his little friends.

Once a year, the poor children of Cleveland have a picnic. The day before the picnic, the man who saves pennies, opens his iron bank and finds the hundreds of pennies that he has saved during the year. The next day, the man goes to the children's picnic and he carries his pennies in a wooden box.

When the children see their friend, they shout and yell, "Here comes the Penny Man! Here comes the Penny Man!" Then the children run and crowd about the smiling miser with his famous box of pennies.

The man takes the cover off his box and throws pennies in all directions. Of course, there is a wild scramble. The children shout and laugh as they try to catch the pennies and pick them off the ground. The penny scramble lasts for some time, until the box is empty, and by that time, every boy and girl has a good number of precious pennies.

Each year the children watch for the Penny Man. They know that he will always come to their picnic. They know, too, that the Penny Man will always have plenty of pennies for all of them. Never once has the Penny Man disappointed the children. He is always on the job making children happy, and making himself happy, too, with his box of pennies.

Children, do you know that the Penny Man acts very much like God? Oh, I don't mean that God saves pennies and throws them away to little boys and girls. But I do mean that God has saved a lot of grace for each one of you. When God died on the Cross on that first Good Friday, He did something good. In fact, God's death on the Cross was the greatest thing that ever happened. Now, God should have received a great amount of grace for dying on the Cross, but God didn't need that grace. God could get into heaven without that grace. So what did God do? God saved the grace that He earned by dying on the Cross, and He saved that grace for you. Any time you want some of that grace, you can have it. You can have that grace by receiving the sacraments.

God gives you grace through the sacraments. Every time you receive one of the sacraments, you receive grace in your soul. You don't have to wait a whole year to receive some of God's grace. Oh, no! If you receive Holy Communion every day, you receive some of God's grace every day. If you go to confession once a week, you receive grace once a week. Yes, every time you receive one of the sacraments, you receive grace. God made the seven sacraments to help you obtain grace.

Boys and girls, you need grace for your soul, and you can never have too much grace. God's grace will buy your way into heaven. That's why you should try to receive as much grace as possible. That's why you should go to confession and receive Holy Communion often. If you receive these sacraments often, you will find it easy to get to heaven.

The children at the picnic try hard to get the Penny Man's pennies. You should try hard to get God's grace by receiving the sacraments often.

––––––––––

This poem is from Sister M. Josita Belger's book, *Sing a Song of Holy Things*, The Tower Press, 1945, page 86.

"Sin"

Sin is such a bad, bad thing;
It spots my soul of white,
And makes it very ugly
In God's most holy sight.

A mortal sin would kill my soul,
And take away God's grace;
Venial sins are evil, too,
And ugly marks there trace.

I must not spot this soul of mine,
So lovely, pure and bright,
But keep it for God only,
In beauty, shining white.

––––––––––

Discussion Questions

1. How does it help to see your soul as a star?
2. What does it mean to be a miser of grace? What can you do to store up grace in your soul?
3. Why do you think Jesus gave us the great gift of the Sacrament of Penance?
4. What does the story of St. Jerome tell us about what Jesus wants from us? How can this story help

you to participate in the Sacrament of Penance and
Reconciliation often?
5. In your own words, tell what the story of the Penny
Man teaches us about grace. What is your plan for
receiving more grace?

Prayerfully read through Section II of "A Gospel Examination of Conscience" beginning on page 148. End this
session with an Act of Contrition or a prayer of your
own creation.

Lesson Three
Sin

YOU OUGHT BY THIS TIME, my dear children, to know and understand what a sacrament is and what particular kind of a sacrament Penance is. You know the definition by heart; your teachers have explained it many times, and the whole of the last instruction was taken up in trying to make all this clear to you. Every sacrament brings grace to the soul that receives it. When you were baptized, some six or seven years ago, a very great grace was given to you. You were brought here as little babes to the church in a state of original sin. It was no wrong you had done yourselves. You were simply born with that sin. No sin can ever enter heaven. If you had died on your way to the church, or at any time before being baptized, you would have always been outside the gates of that beautiful place where the angels are. But, thank God, you are baptized.

What grace did you receive? That sin I speak of, and which we call original, and with which everyone is born, that sin was washed away. Your soul became pure in the sight of God, you were made His children and He gave you a right to enter the kingdom of heaven. If you had died a year ago, or two or three or more years ago, your souls would have gone at once into where God and the saints are. When you are grown up—I mean when you reach the age of reason, as it is called —then you run the risk of committing a mortal sin. As long as you are in that mortal sin, as long as it remains with you, you are in great danger of being lost forever—of never seeing God.

I like to think that all you boys and girls have not done any serious wrong. I like to believe, and I think I am right in believing it, that most Catholic boys and

41

girls come to their seventh year, or tenth for that matter, without willingly saying or thinking or doing anything that it is not permitted by the commandments to say or to think or to do. From what I know of children, I really feel certain that a great many of them so live during the days of their early childhood that if they were to die without the chance of seeing the priest their souls would not be lost. Those souls of theirs might have to stay a little while in Purgatory, but they would sooner or later enter into the kingdom of heaven. I am sure that while I am talking to you I am looking at many who have not so far been guilty of a mortal sin. Is not that a beautiful way to live? Would it not be splendid to live that way all your lives, no matter if your lives were to last one hundred years? You can do it. I wish you to pray that that may be the fruit of your first confession. I wish you, every time you think of that confession, to say to yourselves that with God's help you will never do anything that might be a mortal sin as He has been so merciful as to pardon you everything and has given you a chance to begin all over again.

It is well for you to have some idea of what sin is. You must try to understand that sin is the worst thing that can happen in your life. It is worse than all the

> Sin is the worst thing that can happen in your life.

suffering you can think of. It is worse than being poor or sick or dying. I mean it does you more harm than any of these things. I mean it would be better for you to have and to let all these things happen to you than to commit one sin, even one venial sin.

What is sin? You know that it is something wrong, something you should not do. But your catechism tells you more about sin than that. Your catechism tells you that sin is any willful thought or word or deed or omission against the law of God or against the law of the

Church. You will notice in the first place that you can do wrong in four ways. You can do wrong by thinking wrong, by saying wrong, by doing wrong and by omission; that is, by not doing what the commandments tell you to do.

You must remember that in order to commit a sin you must be free. You must, moreover, know that what you are doing is wrong. Do not forget this. You must be free. If you are not free no matter what you do there is no sin. It is a sin to steal; but, suppose now, somebody would take your hand in spite of you—that is, against your will—and force you to put it into somebody's pocket and take out of that pocket some money, would you in that case be guilty of theft? Certainly not. Why? Because you did not do that act of stealing of your own free will. Somebody else made you do it.

Two things are necessary for every sin. If either one of those two things is missing, you do not commit a sin. You must know that what you are doing is wrong. If you do not know that it is a sin, no matter what it is, it is not a sin for you. Sometimes a child walks in its sleep. A child like that might set the house on fire. To burn down a house and de-

> We need never fall into sin unless we wish to.

stroy some lives would, beyond doubt, be a very great sin. But the child does all this in his sleep; does it become guilty of an awful crime? No. Why? Because the child, being asleep, did not know what he was doing, and so, though great harm followed his act, yet because he was not aware of what he was doing there was no sin at all. You see that in one way it is easy and in another way it is hard to commit a sin. It is well to know that we need never fall into sin unless we wish to.

There are two kinds of sin. There is original sin, that is, the sin in which everyone is born. Original sin we do not commit—it is not something we do ourselves.

It is a state in which we come into the world. It is like being born blind or deaf or lame. But we must get rid of it in order to become a child of God and have a right, if we do as we should, to go to heaven.

Baptism, the first sacrament—which all who wish to be saved must receive—gives us that grace, changes the state of the soul and makes it fit to see God. Without Baptism, you cannot receive any of the other sacraments, because as long as we are in the original sin we are not members of the Church and so the sacraments are not for us. Baptism opens the gate to the other sacraments and all the blessings of the Church.

Besides original sin, there is actual sin. Actual sin is the sin we commit ourselves of our own free will. It is the sin of which we make ourselves guilty when we know that what we are doing is wrong, and, knowing that, do it of our own accord, in spite of the commandments. There are two kinds of actual sin; there is only one kind of original sin. The two kinds of actual sin are called mortal and venial. The actual sin, which is called mortal, is that sin which is a very serious act against the law of God. When I say act I mean not only a deed, or what we do, but I mean as well a thought or a word, for you must never forget that in four ways you may break God's holy law.

The four ways are by thought, by word, by deed, and by omission. You do wrong by omission when you do not do what is ordered by the law of God; for example, if you do not go to Mass on Sunday or holy days of obligation, the sin is a sin of omission, because you refuse to do what has been commanded by God and by the Church. Now a mortal sin is a very great sin. It is called mortal, because if one dies in mortal sin the soul is dead; that is, is lost forever. Mortal sin is the worst thing that can happen to you or to any one in this world. Keep that in your minds always. This thought will keep you on your guard the whole time, and you will do all that is in your power to not be guilty of mortal sin.

Every morning you must say to yourselves: There is one thing I am not going to do today, and that one thing is, I am not going to fall into mortal sin. You will pray for this great grace daily. Always remember that with God's grace—and your own strong will—nothing in this wide world will be able to make you commit a mortal sin.

> Do all that you can during these days to be perfectly ready.

There was a queen of France, and many and many times she used to say to her young son, who became king and also a saint, "My child, you know how much I love you. I love you so much that I would willingly give up my life for you. Yet much as I love you I would sooner see you fall dead now at my feet than to have you commit one mortal sin." This lesson repeated and repeated had a strong and lasting effect on the young prince. He remembered his mother's words all the days of his life, and he hated mortal sin more than sickness or suffering or death.

Once more I ask you to think how wonderful a thing the Sacrament of Penance is that, in two or three or five minutes, can take away that awful danger from your souls. But confession does that only when you make it well. So, again, do all that you can during these days to be perfectly ready, so that when you tell all the sins of your very short lives God will be so pleased with your preparation that He will wipe out every stain that may be on your souls, just as you rub out with a sponge all the chalk marks on a blackboard, so that you may begin writing over again. Your souls once made white by confession will be ready for you to put anything on them; they will be ready for you to write good and kind thoughts, beautiful words and splendid deeds. You will make up your minds firmly that there is one thing you will never let into your souls, and that one thing is sin. I cannot tell you how happy that will make you.

Do you know of anything that can make you more glad than to be sure that, no matter how quickly you may die, or when or where or how you may die, your soul will be received into the arms of God your Father and kept in those arms forever? That is the way to live up to the words of the catechism. Why did God make you? God made me to know Him and love Him and serve Him in this life, and to be happy with Him forever in the next. In this way, you will love Him and serve Him in this world, and you will be happy with Him forever in the world that you enter after death. That is the only way to live, and that is the only way to die.

I will have a good deal to say about sin; in fact, I feel that I must say very much about sin, because I want you to hate it with all your hearts. Your catechism asks you how must you love God, and the answer is, "'You shall love the Lord, your God, with all your heart, with all your soul, and with all your mind. This is the greatest and the first commandment.'"[8] There is another greatest and first commandment. It is this: You shall hate all kinds of sin with your whole heart and with your whole soul and with your whole mind. These two commandments are almost one and the same. You cannot love God without hating sin, and it is impossible to hate sin without loving God. So, if you wish to prove to yourselves that you love God, ask yourselves whether you hate sin.

Of course, most of what I have so far spoken has to do with mortal sin. There is another kind of actual sin. It is called venial sin. Venial sin is not as great a sin as mortal sin. It does not bring the soul to hell. If, when

---

[8] Matthew 22:37-38

one dies, one is in the state of venial sin—that is, if one has no mortal sin—then the soul is not lost. The soul in this case will not go to the prison house, from which there is no escape forever, but the soul will have to stay for some time in a place of punishment, which is called Purgatory, and where it will do penance until it is fit to take its place among the blessed in heaven.

To tell a lie, for example, a lie which does harm to nobody, a lie to get out of some trouble, a lie of excuse, is a venial sin. But to utter a falsehood which does damage to somebody's good name would be a mortal sin. To steal a pin or something of very little value would be a venial sin, but to take a large sum from another would surely be something which would offend God greatly, and so be a mortal sin. Every wrong word or wrong act or wrong thought offends our Father who is in heaven, but there are some wrong things which anger Him more than others. That is the reason why some actual sins are called mortal and some venial.

Of course, we should be more on guard against mortal than against venial sin, but the best plan is to make up our minds that nothing in this whole world will be able to force us into any kind of sin. If you were to say to yourselves, my dear children, each one of you, "I will do my best not to fall into mortal sin, but as to venial sin I will not be so careful," I would be afraid that, little by little, you would get nearer the edge of mortal sin and finally tumble in. But if I heard you say, "I am not going to commit any sin at all, not even the slightest," then I would begin to hope that, little by little, you would grow to hate all sin, and that thus you would pass all the days of your life without ever once being obliged to tell in confession a mortal sin, for the simple reason that you kept away from that great evil altogether.

Remember your Maker in the days of your youth, but remember Him with love, and no grievous fault

47

will you ever be blamed for, either by God or by your own souls. Remember your Maker with love and with thanks. He has been so good to you. He has never done you any harm. He made you for Himself. Sometimes there are golden hours and very happy days in this life, but they are nothing to the glad hours and glad days that God is preparing for you in heaven, and which will surely b« yours if you love Him and hate sin.

Discussion Questions

1. Why is sin the worst thing that can happen to you?
2. By what four ways can you commit sin? (Remember when you examine your conscience to always check for sins of omission—those things you should have done and did not do.)
3. Name two things necessary for sin to be committed.
4. Name the two types of sin. How are they different?
5. Explain the difference between mortal sin and venial sin. Which is more serious? Why?

I Talk with God

Read the following prayer by Sister M. Imelda aloud together as you kneel before a crucifix:

Dear Jesus, I know that You will forgive my sins. But I know, too, that You will punish me for my sins. That is only fair. I am sorry for my sins. I do not want to be punished for them. But I have done wrong. I know that sin hurts You, Jesus. I know that it was because of sin that You suffered and died on the Cross. I am sorry for my sins because my sins have hurt You, my Jesus. Amen.

Lesson Three Read-aloud Story and Poem

This is another story from *I Belong to God, Great Truths in Simple Stories for Children and Lovers of Children* by Lillian Clark, Longmans, Green and Company, 1936, pages 27-40.

"When the Children of Men Go Mad (Sin)"

I KNOW meditating means thinking especially of things, but how strange! Am I to think especially today of sin if I thought it was not a nice thing to do, and why should I think so about it? I hate it and—ah! That is it—do you really hate sin and do you hate the place into which it can draw you?

Draw me? . . . Can sin draw me anywhere? It takes powerful machines and electricity to pull me along. I am pretty big; can sin draw me? This is our question today—Let us see just how strong sin is.

Let us pretend that you and I are fairies and that we lived long, long ago before God had made the world or any man or woman or little child at all, when He had made no one but the angels. God was living all alone in His heaven, and the angels were not yet there but were waiting, still waiting just outside, hoping and longing for the minute to go through the pearly gates into the arms of the Father who made them and who loved them so dearly. You know, of course, that when God made the angels they had to prove their right to live in heaven. Let us pretend, even, that we have been invited to— THE FIRST TEST—The Angels' Test.

Do you know what tests are? Certainly you do. You take them at the close of the year to see if you are ready to pass into a higher grade.

So, let's pretend, you and I, that we have gone up, up so very high, up to the highest heavens, and are sitting in our fairy swing ravished and enchanted, and transported out of ourselves, enfolded in the mysterious beauty of creation's fair dawn. We are seated far above the angels' heads, or shall we say wings, and we shall watch their test. We shall see if they are ready; we shall see if they will pass . . . pass higher . . . pass through those lovely gates into the embrace of their waiting Father.

My, how beautiful! . . . The sight almost blinds us with its utter light. Look at the multitude of ravishing spirits—God's radiant, grace-glowing angels. Our hearts flutter with gladness—they are so lovely. It is like watching thousands and thousands of sparkling diamonds or dancing sunbeams, or like the shinings and gleamings of thousands and thousands of sunlit crystals. It is like looking into an endless garden of spotless, white lilies, so pure are these angels; it is as though all the soft and flaming sunsets—all the rosy tints and amber hues that ever could be—were gathered in one place, so warm and ardent and loving are their hearts. And my! But they are happy . . . they dream of heaven, and they long for God. They know the gates are soon to open, and they know their thrones are waiting for them.

But hush! The test begins. All are listening—God Himself gives it—just one question, one simple favor— one only service He asks. An awful moment passes. . . . All is silent.

Quickly the test is done, quickly the answers come. "We will," and "We will not," we hear them say. But what is the disorder—something is happening—the angels are dividing—see, the grand leaders spring forth and line the angels up. . . . A struggle? How awful! Can it be the angels are in battle? . . . Look close. The good "We wills" drive back the "We will nots."

Look, look, oh look! The gates are open. The faithful ones pass in. . . . Songs of love are bursting from their lips. Oh, good! They've passed the test.

But the gates! The gates! They're closing. . . . All are not in. . . . Oh, wait, wait! Oh, hurry! Mercy, can some have failed? . . . We are afraid to look. . . . Ah, yes, the "We will nots."—Their thrones are lost; they've lost their Father—His care, His love—never will they see His face.

Oh sad, sad day—Oh day of darksome horror!

The beauty around us has suddenly vanished—something seems to be slipping. . . . The glorious light is fading. . . . Shadows are falling. . . . The heavens are topsy-turvy, and there is no Mother Mary to call upon. We scarce can see. Quick as a flash they change. . . . Look! Look, our once lovely angels—they seem withered—crooked—twisted—bent—and ugly.

Quick as a flash they stir. . . . They move. . . . Oh dreadful! Dreadful! Angels in ruins—everlasting cinders now, like angry streaks they fall. We dare not look. Our hands cover our eyes. . . . Where, where will they stop? . . . You know where. . . . You know where the bad angels went forever—for evermore.

"What drew them there?" you answer. Was it electricity? Or machines? Ah no—sin—only sin can change God's angels into devils and send them hurling into hell.

THE SECOND TEST—

Now let us leave our fairy swing (but we are fairies still, let us pretend) and we are invited to the second test. Where will this be? Think hard. . . Who took it? You know—Adam and Eve, so it will be in the Garden of Eden, of course. We shall watch this time from our gossamer nest in the top of a towering tree. . . .

How beautiful the world is, fresh from the hand of

God. . . . We sit wrapped in the magic mists of early morning, and we see the day blossom forth like a perfect flower. No dust nor frost has come to spoil its leaves and flowers; no bitter cold nor scorching heat, and of all the new and lovely earth the Garden of Eden is the fairest spot. Never were there such giant roses, never were shy violets sweeter. The leaves are like finest lace —the fruits here are like sugar and rich honey. We hear the musical murmur of the rippling waters; we see the starry eyes of a thousand delicate blossoms, and the lively plumage of the feathered citizens of cloud-topped trees and lowly shrubs. The garden is dancing in a shower of beauty and color and perfume, and into this heaven on earth God put two people—our first parents.

Of all the lovely things there, they are the fairest— fair with the blush of grace. Fairest, because their souls possess God's most precious gift—His own very life. The very blaze of His own beauty is shining within them.

The garden is theirs to do with as they please. . . . My, but they are happy! Calm minds, so clear and peaceful, and hearts bursting with ardent love. No pain; no sorrow; no war; no study; no sickness; no, not even death for when their life on earth is finished. God means to call them home, and they are to rise gently up to heaven just as they are.

And oh! How sweet! Toward evening God comes Himself and walks with them as the sun sets and the dew falls. We can almost imagine we hear them saying, "How good it is to have You, dearest Lord. You are so kind. Our hearts are filled with bliss and burn with warmest love for You."

And then His answer—"It is all yours—animals, flowers, fruits, everything—use it as you wish, but just one little thing I ask, one act to prove your love." They are listening carefully. "Do not eat the fruit of that tree growing there in the center of the garden." This is their test. How easy! They'll pass; heaven is sure to be theirs.

But alas! Who is crawling in under the trees? Who indeed?—The serpent, the Devil, the leader of the fallen angels. He is so angry with himself, so jealous of Adam and Eve, and so afraid they will have his lost throne. See, he is speaking to Eve. . . . Oh! Hear the lies he tells her. . . . Hear him coaxing, tempting her.

O Mother Eve, do not listen. Run, run away and say a little prayer, and God will set all right. Oh, do not stay. Must God be disappointed again? Will He lose these two lovely creatures as He lost the angels? Goodness, she is listening; she is answering. . . . How dreadful! She believes his lie. . . . Worse and worse . . . she eats the fruit—and so, alas, does Adam.

The test is done. They've failed. Our hearts are turning sick. Will they change too? The sting of shame leaps into their guilty hearts. Oh, see it covers their cheeks with its blush. . . . It sends the smile from their lips . . . the light from their eyes—their once blissful hearts are breaking. They run; they hide. . . . Like the bad angels they've lost their thrones.

Heaven is closed, and their beautiful souls have become (dare I say it?) a place of death, yes, of fearful death —they have killed God's life there.

Ah, how heartsick they feel! . . . Out from the garden of pleasure, see God's angels driving them. Strangers are they—no more His children. See now what enters into their lives. . . . Like mad, angry dogs breaking their chains, see suffering—pain—grief—sadness— war—weakness—darkness and every other misery bursting into their lives. Thorns, thistles, and nettles crush out the fair flowers; weary days of toil and work begin, and at the end will come chilly death. This is now their lot.

So the second test ends. What made it a failure? "Electricity," "machines," you answer, no, only cruel, mighty sin could change the world like that.

Now forget that you were playing fairies and remember yourself, just as you are. Do you still think that you are too big for sin to draw you? "No, no," you quickly say, "the angels and Adam and Eve were stronger than I am and if sin did such frightful things to them, oh, what can it not do to little me? I am afraid. I have committed sins, maybe big ones. Is my soul dark and lifeless like theirs?

Have I, O my Father, crushed Your very life out of my temple? Have I cut myself off from You? Are You angry with me? Have You turned Your holy face from me? Have I lost my throne too, and is heaven closed to me?

Well, certainly, if you have sinned deeply, it is.

Think hard. Look deep down into your heart and as far back into your life as you can. Since you were a little one, what has been wrong? (Go slowly now)—at home . . . visiting . . . at church, forgetting our Lord and talking . . . in the dining room, kitchen, schoolroom, bedroom. Looking about saying your prayers or missing them; disobeying; lying; stealing; cheating in school; being angry; quarrelling; hitting; answering back; saying naughty words; doing bad things; missing Holy Mass and being late—and all the rest. Oh, if you could see what is written against you in heaven from your first sin until now! How you should hate to have your mother or your friend see that list, and—are you not ashamed? God sees it and His loving heart grows sad. The dear

Virgin Mother Mary, too, has to turn her pure, loving eyes away from your much-stained soul. Do you not hang your head in shame?

"Yes, I am ashamed . . . what shall I do?" You know. You know what you should do. . . . You know you have what the angels and Adam and Eve did not have.

Yes, sweet Jesus, I know. I know I have Your priests, Your Church, Your Sacrament of Penance, your confession. I know You bought these for me by Your bitter Passion and heavy Cross. I know that the night before Your cruel death You went into a mountain and all alone asked Your heavenly Father to let You take my sins upon You, and I know that they covered Your pure soul, and I know too, that they were so heavy, and so many, that they threw You to the ground in a great agony of pain and misery. I know that You did all this because You love me, and that it is in Your Precious Blood that my darkened, spotted soul will be bathed in confession, and my sins washed away. I shall be whiter than snow.

Ah, Jesus, I was the sinner, but You did the suffering. I know in confession I shall kneel at Your side with Your arm about me and Your dear head bent low to forgive me as soon as I say I am really sorry. Oh, help me with Your light; help me to be very, very sorry; help me to hate bad, wicked sin and never to forget that it is the strongest and most terrible thing in this world, but help me still more to remember that You alone are stronger; that if I ask You, You will save me, for "Savior" means to save and You are my Savior.

(Now, my dear, be very silent and loving. Ask your dear Mother Mary to help you to think of your sins and to make you very sorry because they pain Jesus. Ask Him to help you to hate sin more and more each day.

Always remember in confession if, something troubles you to put it first and to say right off, "Father, I have something that is hard to say," and then the priest will help you and everything will be well.

Now pray a loving Act of Contrition, the Our Father and "O Mary conceived without sin, pray for us who have recourse to Thee."

This poem is excerpted from the book, *Religious Poems for Little Folks,* which is part of the Highway to Heaven reading series by the Bruce Publishing Company, 1936, page 120.

"How Children Should Live"

Let dogs delight to bark and bite,
For God has made them so;
Let bears and lions growl and fight,
For 'tis their nature to;

But children, you should never let
Such angry passions rise;
Your little hands were never made
To tear each other's eyes.

Let love through all your actions run,
And all your words be mild;
Live like the Blessed Virgin's Son,
That sweet and holy Child.
—Isaac Watts

Discussion Questions

1. Do you think either the angels who failed the test or Adam and Eve later thought it was worth it? Is

sin ever "worth it"?

2. What makes sin powerful? Do you think sin can take away your freedom? What can you do to break sin's power over you?

3. What does the poem, "How Children Should Live" teach us? Why is this lesson so hard to live?

Prayerfully read through Section III of "A Gospel Examination of Conscience," which begins on page 149. End this session with an Act of Contrition or a prayer of your own creation.

Lesson Four
Resolution

I WOULD LIKE, my dear children, to do two things for you during these days of preparation for your first confession. It would please me very much and I would give great thanks to God, if I helped you to receive the Sacrament of Penance in the best possible way, and if I coaxed you to make a promise to never commit sin—a promise so strong that nothing in this great, big world could make you break it.

You must pray to obtain these two graces. There is really nothing else which God might give you that would make you so happy as that double grace. There is hardly anything that you cannot do by prayer. But there is something else that will aid you. That one thing is to think. I know that it is not very easy for children of your age to keep your minds upon anything seriously for a long time. But still you may, if you will, do a little thinking. You know yourselves that it is worthwhile to think. You do quite a number of things without thinking. Some of them are not wrong, but some of them are, and you give as an excuse—not seldom, when your father or your mother is offended with you—you give as an excuse that you did what they are questioning you about, without thinking. In fact, you say to yourselves, when you look at some of your actions, that you wonder why you did them, and that if you had thought just for one moment more you would never, never have said such a word or been guilty of such an action. Now you understand why I ask you to think.

I am going to beg of you to think just a very little. I am going to beg of you to think about sin, so that you will always remember that it is the worst thing that can happen to you. Every day of your lives you will be asked to do something that God forbids. The Devil will ask you, and what is called the world will ask you, and sometimes you will desire of your own selves, to commit sin. This means that every day of your life you must fight against this great danger; it means that until you die you will scarcely be free for a single day from the risk of falling into sin. You must therefore prepare for this fight every day. If you begin now to stand up against sin, you will grow braver and braver, so that, in the end, sin will be more afraid of you than you will be afraid of sin. You know that you need never fall into sin unless you will it. You know that your enemy is very strong, but he is never strong enough to beat you against your will. He is very powerful, but he is not more powerful than you with God's assistance. Hence, if you really mean to keep away from sin, God will always be on your side; and you will always win.

> Every day of your life you must fight against sin.

Look at the helpers you have. Look at those who take part in this fight. There you are yourself, and if in the awful moment you pray, at once on your side stand your beautiful guardian angel and your loving mother, the blessed Virgin Mary, and God with His grace; against you there is only the Devil. Now, in a fight like that who ought to win? You say immediately, why, I ought to win. So it is, my dear children. Remember this when you are tempted to do wrong. Remember how many and how powerful are those upon whom you have every right to call; remember that they will be at your side just as soon as they hear your cry. Remember this and do not give way, but be brave soldiers and fight hard, and think that God and Christ and the Queen of Heaven and all the angels are looking down upon you, and that there will be great joy in heaven because you have fought well and won the crown.

You must become more and more sure that there is one thing that you will never let enter your life. I have said it so often that at once you say, that one thing is sin. You see, I am saying many things over and over again. The reason is that I am more anxious than I can tell you to have this thought of mine against sin stick forever in your minds. I wish the hatred for sin—for any kind of sin, for all sin—to be so strong that no matter where or how you see it, you will have so powerful a disgust for it that the very sight of it will not only make you afraid, but really sicken you, so that you will run away from it at once.

I am looking ahead to the future—to your future. You may be all right now, but I have in my mind the days that are to come. I am afraid of those days. I do not know what they will bring you. You know that sometimes children who are very good when they grow up change their lives altogether. They forget their Church and all that their Church bids them do. When younger they never missed Mass on Sundays or holy days of obligation; they always said their morning and their night prayers; they never ate meat on days on which it was not allowed. Their lives are not the same as when they were young—as when they were preparing for their first confession.

What has come over them? They have simply lost their hatred for sin; they are no longer afraid of it. They used to receive Communion weekly and go to confession at least monthly, and now they scarcely go once a year. They used to love to go to the sacraments; they felt so happy after receiving absolution, and now they have lost their taste for all the good practices of their early days, and at last a time comes when they forget their Church altogether, and you know, my dear children, that when they forget their Church, it is the same thing as forgetting God, and you understand that they are running a great risk of never seeing God at all. Can you imagine anything more awful than that?

What brings such a state of things about? That terrible thing will always happen when one begins to lose hatred for sin. You do not wonder, I am sure, when I tell you all these things about sin; you do not wonder why I am all the time begging you to ask God to make you feel toward sin as you feel toward disease. When you stop hating sin, you begin to love it. You know how dangerous it is to trust one you know is your worst enemy. You never can tell when such an enemy will lie in wait for you to do you harm. Your worst enemy cannot begin to hurt you as much as sin. Sin can cast you body and soul into hell forever. Sin will hate you as much as you love it. Sin will never spare you. Sin will never have any mercy upon you. Sin will never be satisfied till it makes you its slave. Sin will never stop until it owns you body and soul. Sin wants only one thing, and that is your soul. Sin means only one thing, and that is to keep your soul wretched in this life and prevent it from ever being happy with God in the next.

So you see, sin is your worst enemy. Sin is a murderer. Sin is an assassin, that is, one who kills by a stab in the dark. I cannot say things bad enough about sin. I cannot paint it black enough for you. Have you ever heard of all the harm done by sin? No, my dear children, not all the books in the world would be able to hold all the evil for which we must blame sin. You have been told about the beautiful angels. They were the first creatures God made for Himself. I could not make you understand how bright they are. They are the messengers of God. They come to us from Him, and they go from us to Him. As someone has said in verse:

> **When you stop hating sin, you begin to love it.**

> **Sin is your worst enemy.**

Lesson Four

"Around our pillows golden ladders rise,
And up and down the skies,
With winged sandals shod.
The angels come and go, the messengers of God."

They are more lovely than you can dream of. You
have seen their pictures, but those pictures do not give
you the least idea of how beautiful they are. God did
not place them in heaven at once. It was necessary for
them, as it is for us, to fight their way to perfect happiness. They were to be tried, and if they were found
faithful, then an eternal crown was to be theirs; but if
they were found wanting, then they were to be forever
miserable. The trial God put them to was to them what
a temptation is to us. You know what a temptation is—
something that asks us to do wrong, something that asks
us to break the commandments in some way or other,
something that asks us to disobey God. We know that
we have many temptations. The angels had only one
that in some way or other invited them not to do what
God told them to do, which, in other words, invited them
to commit sin. Nobody knows what kind of a temptation
it was.

Try, my dear children, to let your thoughts go back,
oh, so many years, until you get to that moment when
the trial of the angels took place. They were not yet in
heaven, remember. As I told you, they had to win heav-
en as we have to win it. They had to fight for it as we
have to fight for it. If they had been in heaven they
would have seen God, and once having seen God they
would love Him so much that they could not love anything else but Him, and therefore could not love sin.
Try and make a picture in your own minds of all those
angels. They were so good to look upon. Then there
were so many. Look upon that shining army, bright as
the sun and beautiful as the moon. Think how God,

looking down upon them, must have loved them. Now listen to the order of the Almighty. Possibly St. Gabriel, the archangel, sent the sound of his trumpet through all their ranks and told them what the Lord wished them to do. They heard the command. It must have been something not at all easy to do.

It was so hard that every angel may have halted and wondered. Everyone is fighting with himself. Each one says, will I or will I not obey? It is all done in a second. Many say, I will not serve; the others all say, I will obey because God is not only my Father, but my Master, and whatever He orders must be done.

St. John, the apostle—it was he who wrote one of the four Gospels, and then, in his old age, the last book in the Bible, which is called Revelations, and in which he tells us that he had been carried to the highest heaven, and had been allowed to see the wonderful things therein—the wonderful things not only of the present, but of the past and the future. St John gives us just a little bit of news of that minute which was so full of danger for those angels. Think, if you can, how many were the angels. They cannot be counted; they are more in number than the grains of sand on all the shores of the world; they are more in number than all the drops of all the rivers and lakes and seas and oceans anywhere and everywhere.

Some of those angels would not listen to God. They did what pleased themselves, and did not care whether they did something displeasing to their Maker. They did not know how much they displeased Him. Had they known how angry they made Him, had they known how much their disobedience was to make them suffer, they would never have fallen into their great sin—never. But they did fall. They did commit sin. Their sin was a very great sin; it was a mortal sin. You remember what I told you about mortal sin. Just think of it!

This was the first sin ever committed. It was the first sin God ever saw. Just see what He did when it came before His eyes. It is well always to remember this. As He treated this first mortal sin, He may treat all mortal sins. In fact, as He treated the sin of the angels, so will He deal with the mortal sins of those who die and come before Him without washing away those sins in the Sacrament of Penance. The angels were way above us. They were more perfect than we are. They were pure spirits. They had no bodies and so they could not die. God loves every creature He makes. He loves us, as you know, very, very much; but I feel that He loved the angels even more than He loves us. Think of this. Yet in spite of it, call to mind how terribly He punished them. What did He do to them on account of that one sin?

First, they had no time to tell God how sorry they were for their bad deed. Perhaps they did have time to make an act of contrition, but they were too proud to make it. I like to think that He gave them a chance to become His friends again, but they did not wish to do so. Then His justice fell upon them. What happened? They were at once cast down into hell. He made hell on account of them. They were never to see Him again. He would never smile on them again. They were to be in darkness and pain and fire forever.

Did you ever try to think of the meaning of that word "forever?" How many years is it since they were driven from His love? No one can tell. Suppose it was ten thousand years ago; suppose it was a hundred thousand years ago, or a million years. They have been in hell all that long, long time. They are there now while I am talking to you. All that dreary past does not count for anything. They are just as if they were only at the beginning of

> Did you ever try to think of the meaning of that word "forever?"

their great woe. And they are going to be there forever. That is, their suffering will never end. They are in darkness worse than that of the blackest kind you ever saw or any one will ever see, and no matter how far, in their grief, they look ahead, they will never see the sign of any morning. Never, never, never. They will always be in the dark—always, always, always in the night. No moon, no stars in that blackness.

Why do I say so much about the angels who sinned? Because I want to make you understand what a terrible thing sin is, and how God hates it and how well you must prepare yourself for your confession, so that, like God, you may hate sin more than anything else.

Discussion Questions

1. What is the worst thing that can happen to you? Whom should you call upon in your fight against it?
2. Explain in your own words why you must hate sin.
3. What resolution must you make as you prepare for the Sacrament of Reconciliation?

I Talk with God

Dear Jesus, I know how much my sins have hurt You. I am sorry that I have hurt You. I do not want to hurt You ever again. How can I be sure of not hurting You? I will try very hard never again to sin. But You must help me, dear Jesus. I cannot be good without Your help. Help me, Jesus. I will try very hard to be good. This will show I love You. Amen. (Prayer by Sister M. Imelda)

Older children and adults: Memorize and pray often Pope Leo XII's prayer to St. Michael the Archangel as found on page 145.

Lesson Four Read-aloud Stories and Poem

This story is from *Terrible Farmer Timson and Other Stories* by Caryll Houselander, Sheed & Ward, 1957, pages 105-116.

"Joseph's Godfather"

IF THE BOMB had not fallen in the next street, Joseph might never have known his godfather. For, to tell the truth, he was a very bad godfather indeed. He had never even asked whether Joseph had made his First Communion, let alone sent him a birthday present, or even a picture postcard. Then suddenly, just before the bomb fell, Mother had a letter. She read it out loud and they all laughed. It said:

Dear Margaret,

I suppose you know that I now live in England at the above address. You had better send your child to me for the duration.

Arthur

Mother made excuses for him, but then she always made excuses for everyone. "He has been shooting tigers in India for years," she said, "miles from a church, and so I am afraid he has become a little odd. He may even have given up going to Mass."

"That's a fine sort of godfather for me," said Joseph.

"You must pray for him," Mother answered.

And then, the very next night, the bomb fell. "That settles it," said Mother. "Joseph must accept his godfather's invitation."

"What!" said Joseph, "go and live till the war ends with an old man who is odd and doesn't even go to Mass!"

67

"You are ten years old," Mother answered, "and a soldier's son, old enough to go to Mass and act sensibly yourself. You must pray for your godfather. Of course, it's going to be hard. You may feel very lonely and strange at first. Godfather is used to being treated like a little tin god in India; he won't like any smart answers, you know, but you must be brave and act like a man. Try to offer it all up for Godfather."

The afternoon when Joseph arrived at his godfather's house was the most unhappy one he had ever spent. Although the cook was kind and motherly and sat him down to a nice supper by the kitchen stove, he had a sinking feeling in his stomach. The food turned to ashes in his mouth, and he felt the tears he was determined not to shed making his throat sore.

"What's Godfather like?" he asked miserably.

Before Cook could answer anything, Singh, the Indian manservant, who was cleaning a pair of Godfather's shoes, answered, "He is a very fine gentleman, a *pukka Sahib*."

"What's that?"

"Bless your heart!" said Cook. "You don't know what a *pukka Sahib* is? Why, it means a great gentleman, and that's just what the General is."

"Is Godfather a general?"

Singh said proudly, "He is a *great* general; all the soldiers tremble when he speaks, and tigers run away."

Just then the bell rang and Singh went to answer it. He came back for Joseph. "The general wants to see you," he said.

Joseph took hold of Singh's hand and held it till they got to the door. He felt much more frightened than he did of bombs, and longed for Mother. At the door he said,

"I'll go in alone."

It was as bad as he expected. His godfather stood before the fire on a tigerskin rug—a tall, straight, white-haired, bristling old gentleman with a mustache twisted into spikes like two daggers, a monocle in one eye, a very large, very red nose, and eyebrows that bristled out over his fierce blue eyes like the antennae that Joseph had photographs of in his nature books.

"How do you do, sir," said Joseph politely.

"How do I do, eh? Ha! That's a good one. How do I do?" Godfather gave a roar of savage laughter, and Joseph, who could not see anything funny in his greeting, trembled.

"How do I do, ah, ah, ah! I do fine; I take good care I do. How do *you* do, that's the point. Let's see you. Come here."

"Thank you, sir, I'm very well."

"Stuff and nonsense, don't answer me back! Very well! Upon my word, you look half starved." He screwed his monocle so tightly into his eye that it looked as if he were grinding it into his face, and peered more closely at Joseph. "I've never seen such a weedy child," he shouted. "You look like something someone grew in a cellar—a white radish, or a carrot someone pulled up too soon. I suppose you don't take any exercise, eh? Play polo?"

"Play what, sir?"

"Polo, are you deaf? Don't you ride horses?"

"No, sir."

"Frightened of 'em, eh?"

"No, sir."

"Don't answer me back, I tell you. I wouldn't put up with it from a tiger or a cannibal or from a regiment of soldiers. Bah! It's mutiny, that's what it is!"

Joseph soon got friendly with Cook and the Indian, Singh, and had plenty of fun riding the pony. And though Godfather roared and spluttered at him, he gave him presents every day, didn't send him to school, let him stay up late for dinner. In fact, he spoiled Joseph so much that he began to be fresh to Cook, and to quarrel with Singh (though he was his greatest friend), to be choosy about his food, and worst of all, to find it really rather boring to say his prayers. One day he had to say to himself, "I'm being a rotten Catholic!" and he resolved to make sacrifices for Godfather, and to make sure by keeping a list of them. "That will make me do it, or else," he said. He asked Cook if Godfather ever went to Mass.

"Bless you, he hasn't set foot in church many a year," she said.

The rest of this story has to be told from the general's point of view. To tell you the truth, he liked Joseph better every day, and one day he was looking out of the window watching him ride his pony and feeling rather proud of him, when he caught sight of what he thought was Cook's shopping list dropped on the floor. He picked it up and started to read it. He frowned, twirled his mustache, stared, said, "What the—? Why the—?" and read it all over again.

"Sacrifices for Godfather, to convert him," he read. "Didn't answer back. Ate stewed pears, which I hate. Didn't have lemonade, which I love."

The next day Joseph found Singh and Cook worried. "The Master's sick," said Singh. "He's gone mad."

"And wouldn't touch a nice little chicken I served for his supper last night," said Cook.

"And him drinking cold water, not whiskey and soda," said Singh.

"Take his shoes to him," Cook said, "and ask him where he hurts."

Singh was gone a long time. He came back more worried than ever. "Master's gone mad," he said sadly. "I dropped the best Chinese china dog and broke it. The Master, he turned red, he opened his mouth to roar, and no roar came out. He shut his mouth, struggled as if he had a pain, and said nothing at all!"

"*You* go, Joseph," said Cook, and she began dabbing her eyes and sniffing. "Sounds as if his end is coming."

Joseph went straight up to Godfather's chair. He was not nervous of him now. "Godfather, please tell me what's up. Cook and Singh think you are dying. You aren't eating chicken or drinking whiskey and soda, and you aren't swearing and shouting or anything. If you're dying, you'd better call the priest, because we love you, and we don't want you to go to hell."

All of a sudden, Godfather began to laugh, but not very loud. It was more like giggling, and his face looked like a little boy's who has been caught in something silly. He got Joseph's sacrifice list, all crumpled up, out of his breast pocket, smoothed it out on his knee, and said, "See this?"

Joseph did, and he went as red as a geranium. "Yes, sir," he said.

"Well, I've been trying to see if I could do, for myself, as much as *you* are doing for me. You see? I think it's very decent of you, and by Jove, boy, I can't keep it up! I haven't even started on stewed pears—the things make me sick. Ugh! Why, tigers and cannibals are easy to keep down compared to the old Adam in me. I give it to you, Joseph. You've got more pluck than I have."

"Oh, no, sir," Joseph said, "what rot. I mean, sir, I'm awfully sorry, it's *not* rot. But you see, I can do sacrifices because I go to the Sacraments of Confession and Communion, and so our Lord is in my soul and he helps me. I couldn't do them myself, *by* myself, not even easy ones like those are!"

"Easy! By gad, easy!" Poor Godfather had bellowed again. He clapped his hand over his mouth.

That evening, Joseph went to confession. He got there early and was first in the line. It was a fairly long one, and when he came out he saw something very surprising. The last one in the line was Godfather. He was crouching down looking rather funny, like a naughty boy again, with the collar of his coat turned up around his ears. Joseph pretended not to see him, but after his penance he said a huge thanksgiving.

That night when Joseph, very brushed and washed, came in to dinner, he was surprised to see that there were silver bowls of flowers on the table and everything spread for a feast. Godfather was beaming. He was pouring out some lemonade for Joseph.

"Joseph," he said, "tonight we are having a little celebration. I've gone and done it: gone to confession, by Jove. I feel a different man. So I am, too. We'll have stewed pears another day; it's a feast tonight."

And what a feast it was! First, Singh came in grinning with fried chicken on a silver dish. Then he brought in a bowl heaped high with a mound of mashed potatoes, a pat of rich, yellow butter melting in the middle, and fresh green peas from Cook's garden. Cook had baked her special biscuits, large and crisp, and had made a salad of apples, nuts and grapes. But best of all was the dessert; a feathery-light angel food cake with chocolate icing, and three different kinds of ice cream—vanilla, strawberry, and chocolate.

———————

The following short story, "Joseph in Danger," comes from *Children's Retreats* by Rev. P.A. Halpin, 1926, page 166.

THE PATRIARCH JOSEPH, when a young man, was one day, without any fault on his part, in a dangerous occasion of sin. Someone came up to him suddenly and asked him to do what would offend God. Joseph saw the danger at once, and, without as much as speaking, ran off as fast as he could. The tempter ran after him and seized him by the coat to bring him back. But Joseph, throwing off his coat, ran away, leaving it in the hands of the person who was tempting him, and in this way he escaped the danger.

O my child, how many have fallen into sin because, instead of flying away as Joseph did, they remained in the danger. Be not foolish like them, but rather imitate the saints who are now safe with God because they always ran away when they saw themselves in danger of offending Him.

———————

The following story, "A Piece of Clay" is adapted from Rev. Gerald T. Brennan's *The Ghost of Kingdom Come,* Bruce Publishing Company, 1941, pages 42-51.

Old Benjamin Adams spent his whole life making statues. He made them all out of clay. He made statues of dogs, elephants, tigers—why, Benjamin could make anything with a piece of clay. Day after day, he worked in his shop. With his tiny knife and his piece of clay, old Benjamin was happy—happy as he made his figures from his piece of clay.

Benjamin had three sons—Milton, Bernard, and Roy. For years Benjamin had worked for his sons. He loved his sons. Soon they would be men, and Benjamin was getting old.

One night they were all seated at table—old Benjamin, and his sons, Milton, Bernard, and Roy. When the meal was finished, Benjamin looked at his boys and asked them a question.

"My sons," asked the old man, "do you love me?"

The boys raised their heads.

"Father," they said, "you know that we love you."

Old Benjamin listened and nothing more was said that night about the question.

Another night soon after, old Benjamin and his sons were seated at table. Once again, Benjamin asked his sons, "My sons, do you love me?"

The boys were surprised. "Why certainly, Father," they said, "we love you more than any other children ever loved their father."

The three boys wondered why their father asked such strange questions. Maybe, they thought, he is getting old and cannot think so well any more.

Two weeks later, old Benjamin repeated his question to his three sons: "My sons, do you love me?"

The boys looked at their father—then, at one another.

"Why, Father," they said, "three times you have asked us this question, and for the third time we give you the same answer. You know that we love you. Why do you keep asking us this strange question?"

Old Benjamin Adams arose from his chair.

"My sons," he said, "you have answered well. Three times I have asked you, and three times you have told me that you love me. Now, I am going to give you a chance to prove to me that you love me."

The old man pushed aside his chair. Slowly he left the room. He passed through the hall. He climbed the stairs and entered his shop. In the corner of the room on a table was a large lump of clay. Benjamin picked up the clay, carried it down the stairs, and placed the clay on the table before his three sons. Then he took a large knife. He cut the clay into three pieces. To each son old Benjamin Adams gave a piece of clay.

"My sons," he said, "you have told me of your love. Now prove to me that you love me. Take your piece of clay and make it into my picture. Make a statue of me with your piece of clay. Then I shall know that you really love me."

Each son took his piece of clay. All three boys promised to make a beautiful statue of old Benjamin, their good father.

Milton took his piece of clay and placed it in a drawer. He went off to play.

Bernard took his piece of clay and began to work. He worked for a day or two. Then he grew tired. After all, he thought, there is no need to rush. There is plenty of time. And so, Bernard pushed the clay aside and he, too, went off to play.

Roy took his piece of clay and began to work. For days and weeks, he worked and worked—making a picture of his father from his piece of clay. Oh, it was beautiful when it was finished. His statue looked just like old Benjamin Adams. Roy was very happy.

Months and months passed. Old Benjamin Adams said nothing. He watched and waited.

Finally, one night the old father looked at his sons. He spoke quietly and asked the three sons to bring to him their pieces of clay made into his picture.

Milton ran upstairs, opened the drawer, and there was the clay. It was hard and stiff.

Try as he did, he could do nothing with the clay. It had turned into stone. He was sorry. He was sad.

Bernard took his piece of clay. He had never finished the statue. The clay was dried out; it was a hard, ugly, piece of stone. It was too late to do anything more.

Milton and Bernard showed the horrible pieces of clay to their old father.

"We are awfully sorry, Father," they pleaded.

"So am I," said the old father, "awfully, awfully sorry."

Then Roy came to his father. Roy placed on the table a beautiful statue of his father, a perfect picture of old Benjamin Adams. Roy had worked hard to change the clay into a beautiful picture of his father.

Old Benjamin Adams was happy.

"Roy, my son, you have done well. You have proven to me that you love me. From a piece of clay, you have made a picture of the one you love."

The father took the statue. He placed it on a shelf that all might see it. He stood before the statue and admired it. He loved it.

"This statue," the old man said, "I will always keep before me. It is proof that my son, Roy, really loves me."

And all through the years Benjamin Adams kept the statue before him. He loved to look at it. The statue told him of Roy's love—the love of a son—a son who, from a piece of clay, made a picture of the father he loved.

Application: God, like old Benjamin Adams and his pieces of clay, gives us all a body and a soul. God asks us to take our body and soul and make a picture of God out of them. God says that if we really love Him, we should try to become like Him, and do what He wants us to do.

Most people are like Benjamin Adams' two sons who let their pieces of clay turn into stone. The people who make their body and soul look like God are the people who really love God best. The people who make their pieces of clay into a picture of God—those who really make their body and soul look like God—are also the people whom God loves best.

———————

The following is another poem is from the book, *Religious Poems for Little Folks,* by the Bruce Publishing Company, 1936, page 113.

"Little Things"

Little drops of water
Little grains of sand,
Make the mighty ocean
And the pleasant land.

Thus the little minutes,
Humble though they be,
Make the mighty ages
Of eternity.

Thus our little errors
Lead the soul away
From the path of virtue
Off in sin to stray.

Little deeds of kindness,
Little words of love,
Make this earth an Eden,
Like the heaven above.
—Julia A. F. Carney

Discussion Questions

1. In Lesson Four we learned of the need to hate sin and the importance of our resolution never to commit sin. In "Joseph's Grandfather," we see how important it is to also hate the sins committed by others. What can you, like Joseph, do to help others return to the Sacrament of Penance?
2. "Joseph in Danger" teaches us the importance of avoiding the "occasion of sin." What do we mean by the "occasion of sin"? What practical means can you apply to avoid sin in this way?
3. To live out the lesson the story, "A Piece of Clay," teaches us, what must we resolve to do? List several ways you can do this. What tools will help you keep your resolution?

Prayerfully read through Section IV of "A Gospel Examination of Conscience" beginning on page 150. End this session with an Act of Contrition or a prayer of your own creation.

Lesson Five
Preparing for Confession

I MIGHT TELL YOU a good deal more about sin, but I think that what I have said of the harm it did the angels is enough to help you make up your minds that you will keep away from it all the days of your lives. We can never thank God enough for being so good as to give His Church that great Sacrament of Penance, in which every sin may be washed out and our souls made strong enough to fight against all our enemies. Once more, you see the need of preparing yourself in the best way possible. I feel that at this moment you are, all of you, sure that you are going to do your best. What I have been so far trying to do for you is to make you hate sin, for I know if you hate it, either you will never fall into it, or if you do you will be very sorry for having done so. The first thing now necessary is that you must be sorry for all the sins you may have committed up to now. If when you go to confession you are sorry—really sorry—that is, if you have contrition for your sins, then I have not the slightest doubt that you are going to make a good, indeed a very good, confession.

I wish to talk to you now about the way in which you are always to prepare yourselves for this sacrament. Sometimes on confession days you will see boys and girls rushing into the church, kneeling down for a minute or so, and then, if there is a chance, running right into the confessional. You would certainly say that these children were not really ready to receive the grace of that sacrament as they should. I wish to put you on your guard against this. I wish you, right from your very first confession, to get into the way of doing things as you ought to. If there is anything you must do with care, it is the preparation, not only for your first, but for all your confessions.

In this instruction, I will speak to you about the way in which you are to go about getting ready. When you come into the church on the day you are to make your first confession, kneel down and ask God, through the most Sacred Heart of Jesus and through the Immaculate Heart of Mary, to give you the grace first to know all your sins and then to be sorry—very sorry from the bottom of your heart—for all of them, even the smallest. That is the same as begging for the two-fold favor of making a good examination of conscience and of making a very sincere act of contrition. This you must pray for every time you are about to confess. Then comes the examination of conscience. To examine your conscience means to look over all your thoughts, words, and actions—to find out which were wrong and how many times they were wrong. Never forget that in confession you must tell the priest not only what sins you committed, but also the number of times you were guilty of each offense.

Pray for the grace to know your sins and to be sorry.

There are many ways of examining your conscience, some of which I like and some of which I do not like at all, but which, on the contrary, I detest. You must not think that you have to read the questions which some prayer books have in their pages, in which they try to teach you how to prepare yourselves for the sacrament. Take my advice and never use a prayer book for this purpose. You know that only that is a sin which is against any of the commandments of God or of the Church. So I would say that the easiest and the best way to examine your conscience is to take up the first commandment and ask yourselves whether knowingly and willingly you have ever done anything, or said anything, or even thought anything, against that commandment, and if so how many times. Do the same with the second commandment, and all the other commandments of God, as well as with the first, second, third and fourth precepts of the Church.

There is another way which you might like as well or perhaps like better. You have duties all the time and everywhere. The only time when the commandments do not oblige you is when you are asleep. Otherwise, no matter where you are, you are always obliged to obey. This obligation to do as God's law bids is called your duty. You may, therefore, ask yourselves, "Have I done my duty to everybody—to God, to my parents, to my friends, to my teachers, to all who are in any way my superiors? If not, how many times have I failed?"

As you go along, try to remember so that when you go into the confessional you will not keep the priest waiting. When you have examined your conscience, when you know what sins you have committed, and how many times, then do your best to be really sorry for them. There are many reasons why you should be sorry for your sins, and some of these reasons are better and stronger than others. You may regret having done a wrong act, because what you did was not nice and the thought of it makes you feel ashamed of yourself. Or you may regret because you were found out and your parents or your teachers punished you, or your friends laughed at you or avoided you. Now to be sorry in that way, though it may help you a little to be better in the future, will be of no use in confession. If that is the only kind of contrition you have—if you are sorry for no other reason—then, no matter what else you do, the forgiveness of the priest will not wipe out your sins. That sorrow is useless because it is being sorry—not for your sins—but for yourselves.

Again, you may be sorry because you are afraid of God and of His punishments. You know that He is just and that He hates sin and will punish it as He will also reward virtue. There is hell for those who die in mortal sin, and there is heaven for those who die in the state of grace. If you regret having sinned because it put you in God's anger and in the danger of losing heaven and being condemned to hell, then this regret when it is felt in confession will, with the absolution, remove all stain of guilt from your soul.

But there is a better sorrow. I might call it the sorrow of grateful children who grieve that they have sinned because they have in that way offended God, who has done so much for them, who has given them so many favors, who made them so that they might live in happiness with Him forever, who has forgiven them so many times, who when they were lost by original sin brought them back to His friendship, who is protecting them every second of each hour, who made them members of His Church, who sent down His Son to die for every one of them, who has done so much in the past and is willing to do so much, even much more, in the future for them. If you weep over your sins for all this goodness of God, then your sorrow is of the right kind and with it you will most certainly come from confession with God's love in your souls and with every speck brushed away.

This last kind of contrition is real contrition. The first does not even deserve the name of contrition. The second is just barely contrition, but, remember this, because it is of a low degree of sorrow, it is called not contrition, but attrition.

There is a fourth degree of sorrow for sin. It is that sorrow which leaves ourselves out of sight altogether. It is that sorrow for sin on account of God Himself, because sin has offended One who is so good in Himself, who ought to be reverenced and loved because He is the first and best of all beings, and deserves, without any fear of punishment or hope of reward, to be loved on account of what He is in Himself. Perhaps it is not easy to be sorry in this last manner, yet it is possible and it is this kind of contrition that we should always try to make ours, not only when we go to confession, but every time we examine our conscience or, in any other way, think of our sins.

This sorrow that I speak of now is so powerful that of itself, without going to confession, it is mighty enough to free us from all our sins. It is so wonderful that if we were to die after making such an act of sorrow we would soon be face to face with God and forever. It is worth-while trying to be sorry in this way, and it is above all worthwhile to ask God to give us this grace. The saints had it. There was nothing they hated as much as sin, because there was no one they loved as much as God, and they loved Him for Himself. What

Pray for the grace of perfect contrition.

hatred of sin must have been theirs when they would suffer anything—here or in the world to come—rather than offend God.

There was St. Francis de Sales, whose soul was on fire with the love of God to the degree that once, when the Devil was tempting him to give up all hope of ever seeing God, he prayed that if he was going to be lost, at least he might be allowed to love God throughout his eternal separation from Him. He cared for God and God only, and no matter where he was to be he wanted to love God. Such a love could make acts of perfect contrition only. The lives of the saints are full of such examples.

I find it out of my power to tell you how much of the fruit of your confession depends on your act of contrition. It is not necessary for you to *feel* sorry. What is necessary is to *be* sorry, and you are sorry when you have made up your mind, either through fear or through love of God never to commit sin again. Understand that nobody can make you commit sin in spite of yourself. Understand also, that if you will, you can take a stand against all sin, and that forever. Yes, the grace of God is needed, but you may be sure of this one thing, that if you do all that you are able to do of yourself, God will be at your side ready to help you.

So, before going into confession, ask yourselves whether you are determined, through all difficulties, to keep away from every sin. Be sure of it, inasmuch as you can, and fight as hard as you can with yourself in order to force yourself to take that resolution. You might help yourself to that by looking at your sins, whatever they are, and asking yourselves a few questions about them. You might ask yourself, "Are those things that I have to tell to the priest things to be proud of? Would I want the whole world to know about them?" Yet God knows about them and your angel guardian saw you perform them. You might ask yourselves whether those sins did you any good at all in any way. Perhaps there was more trembling about them than pleasure, perhaps they left a bad taste behind them. I want you to think of anything that will enable you to see how foolish you are when you do wrong, so that for the future you will be on your guard against making a fool of yourself in this way.

Besides, what do you do every time you break a commandment? You offend God. And now ask yourselves what has God done against you that you should so displease Him? Has He hurt you in any way? Rather has He not been good to you in every way? He has kept you alive, watched over you in a thousand ways you know nothing about, protected you against the most terrible accidents and proved to you that He wishes you well. He has been goodness itself. And yet, you would not obey Him. What was His desire when He ordered you to keep His commandments, when He forbade you to sin? Was He thinking only of Himself? Not at all, my dear children. He was thinking of you. He made those commandments in order that by keeping them you might make your lives beautiful, because it was better for you in this world to keep them than to break them, but chiefly because if you acted against them you would run the risk of never being happy with Him in eternity, but of being always unhappy.

The more you think the more clearly you will learn that there is nothing in sin worthwhile, that you cannot give one single good reason or excuse for your sinning. You will find, on the contrary, that in sinning you have been your own worst enemy, while God, in making it a law that you should avoid sin, has been your truest friend. And yet you have gone to work and almost despised this only real friend of yours, the One who was thinking of you and your happiness while you ate and drank and played, during the daytime and also during the night while you were asleep, the One who had you in His mind always, even when everyone else did not even give a thought to your welfare.

> In sinning you have been your own worst enemy.

The surest way of keeping out of sin is to be sorry for it in your heart. It is for this reason I have spent so much time talking to you about contrition. This is why in preparing yourself for confession, you should take more time in making yourselves sorry for your sins than in any other part of your preparation. You may be sure that if you do this, your confessions will make you better and better, until you will come so to hate sin that not all the temptations in the world will be able to lead you away, even the breadth of a hair, from the road of the commandments.

As you get older, and after you have been several times to confession, you will now and then—perhaps often—notice that in spite of all the grace that is contained in this wonderful sacrament for which you are getting yourselves ready, you still commit the same sins and have the same faults to declare to the priest. This will not be a proof that you have made bad confessions but it will show you that though you have had some sorrow for sin, that though you have had enough sorrow to be pardoned, you have not had that great contrition of which I have been speaking, and hence have not got all the profit from the sacrament which God wishes to give you through it.

God, your Father, who is in heaven, not only desires to pardon you all you have done against Him, but He is so good that He is anxious to keep you in His favor always. He does not want you to be for one minute outside His friendship. He loves you so much that He is working all the time to hold you by His side, or rather in His arms. When, therefore, you are asking Him for the grace of a good confession, beg of Him to make your sorrow for your wrongdoing so great that nothing under the sun—nothing—will ever change your firm purpose of never offending Him.

Discussion Questions

1. For what two-fold favor should you pray every time you participate in the Sacrament of Reconciliation?
2. Four types of contrition are discussed in this lesson. In your own words, describe each of these four types of contrition. How can you have perfect contrition (or the fourth degree of sorrow)?
3. "The surest way to keep away from sin is to be sorry for it in your heart." Discuss several ways to do this.

Lesson Five

Fr. Halpin recommends, as one way to examine our conscience, a review of each of the Ten Commandments and the precepts of the Church. Prayerfully review these as outlined in the *Compendium of the Catechism of the Catholic Church* (Part 3, Section Two and the Appendix, respectively.)

Ten Commandments:

1. I am the LORD your God: you shall not have strange Gods before me.
2. You shall not take the name of the LORD your God in vain.
3. Remember to keep holy the LORD'S day.
4. Honor your father and your mother.
5. You shall not kill.
6. You shall not commit adultery.
7. You shall not steal.
8. You shall not bear false witness against your neighbor.
9. You shall not covet your neighbor's wife.
10. You shall not covet your neighbor's goods.

Precepts of the Church:

1. You shall attend Mass on Sundays and on holy days of obligation and remain free from work or activity that could impede the sanctification of such days.
2. You shall confess your sins at least once a year.
3. You shall receive the Sacrament of the Eucharist at least during the Easter season.
4. You shall observe the days of fasting and abstinence established by the Church.
5. You shall help to provide for the needs of the Church.

Additionally, note that the *Compendium of the Catechism of the Catholic Church* states that either perfect contrition (that motivated by love of God) or imperfect contrition (a sorrow for sin that rests on other motives and which includes the determination not to sin again) is an essential element in the reception of the Sacrament of Reconciliation (No. 303).

For very young penitents, Sister Mary Imelda provides a simple examination of conscience:

Did I miss Mass on a Sunday or Holy Day when I could have gone?
Did I laugh at Mass or play at Mass?
Was I late for Mass?
Did I use the Name of God without respect?
Did I disobey my father or mother?
Did I fight or become angry without a good reason?
Did I annoy others?
Did I think, or say, or do, anything impure?
Did I steal anything?
Did I tell a lie?

I Talk with God

Dear Jesus, I have six things to do to make a good confession. First, I must ask the Holy Spirit to help me to know what my sins are. Second, I must try hard to remember what sins I have committed. Third, I must tell God that with all my heart I am sorry I have sinned. Fourth, I must promise God that I will sin no more. Fifth, I must tell my sins to the priest in confession. Sixth, I must do the penance he gives me. Amen.

Act of Contrition: O my God, I am heartily sorry for having offended Thee, and I detest all my sins because of Thy just punishments, but most of all because they offend Thee, my God, who art all good and deserving of all my love. I firmly resolve with the help of Thy grace to sin no more and to avoid the near occasion of sin. Amen.

Lesson Five Read-aloud Stories and Poems

This is another story from *I Belong to God, Great Truths in Simple Stories for Children and Lovers of Children* by Lillian Clark, Longmans, Green and Company, 1936, pages 17-24.

"I Am the Temple of God"
(God in My Soul)

CHARLOTTE, a little girl of five, is going to help today to make you understand what it means when you say, "I am the temple of God."

Last year she spent the Christmas holidays with her aunt who lives in a beautiful house set in the midst of a garden-forest of majestic trees. The little visitor was very welcome, for that household had no children of its own, and her auntie loved her dearly and planned every sort of thing to make her visit pleasant. Sledding and skating and books and dolls and even Christmas parties—besides games of every kind—and Charlotte had a happy, happy time indeed.

But shall I tell you where you would find her when the rising moon was veiling the virgin snow with its silver sheen? Shall I tell you the thing she loved best in this house of her fairy godmother? It was her aunt's jewelry box. At bedtime the child would climb into her aunt's lap, and while she listened to pretty stories of the dear Christ Child, stories of the angels singing in the sky, of the watching shepherds and of the Christmas star, she would pick up one by one the pretty chains and golden rings and sparkling gems, and as her aunt looked on with watchful eye, she would let them fall through her little fingers upon the lovely velvet of the box. She loved to see them shine, and gleam, and make pretty colors in the bright light, and she pretended that they were the Wise Men's gifts to Bethlehem's little King.

"Auntie, of all your jewels which do you like best?" she asked one evening, and her aunt, with a sweet, thinking look, and a warm kiss, answered softly, "This one, dear," and drew out from the lace at her throat, a silken bag. The child's eyes grew big with wonder as she watched her aunt's fingers untie it and take from it a locket no bigger than a penny.

"I love this locket best," she said. "I had it made just so."

"Why, Auntie?"

"Because—because it holds the picture of my boy who is with dear Jesus in heaven." She bravely opened it and looking sweetly out at them was a darling baby face with oh, such a sunny smile and hair all curls and rings.

"Did he look as lovely as that, Auntie?" the child asked as she fondly held him in a tight embrace.

"Yes, it is a perfect likeness, it is his very image, and because I love it so I keep it safely hidden away in this costly locket. I had it made of richest gold and circled round with purest pearls. Protected in this bag, it is safe from every spot and stain. Nothing must dim or mar its golden beauty, because it is my dear boy's little house—his little temple."

They sat for some time quietly musing and drinking in that ravishing breath of heaven. Then Charlotte, returning the smile of the angel-face baby, fell quietly asleep in Auntie's arms.

While Charlotte slumbers, let us put her, Auntie, and baby, gently out of our minds. Now turn your thoughts to yourself and think, "Suppose one day as I kneel all alone praying in my room, I should receive an angel's visit, and he should say to me, 'The good God you pray to loves you dearly. He loves you so dearly, indeed, that He has sent me with this gift to you, it is his own true picture.' 'For me . . . God's own picture for me?' you would stammer, and then, little wondering tears of joy and love would steal into your eyes and you would hardly dare to look upon His holy face. . . . Your heart would melt within you as the angelic messenger continues, 'Lovers of God, good men and women, have painted pictures of Him and put them into churches and holy books, but these are only make-believe pictures. No one before has ever had His picture really— behold, now it is yours."

As the lady did, would you not seek the richest of rich lockets, and would you not wear it round your neck in a strong bag of purest silk? . . . Surely, you would. "Nothing must spot or mar or even touch it; it is God's locket," you would say, and with your eyes closed you would think of the dear face within, and morning, and evening and all through the day, you would whisper words of honeyed love, and little prayers of thanks.

Suppose, you said, but need you be supposing? A greater thing than this has really happened. Listen— "I am God's Locket," you can say, and say too, "my very body is His house—His temple."

Oh! whisper it and say it very, very, softly . . . "Since my baptism, I have carried in my soul God's very likeness, His real image. Yes, even more (dare I say it) the LIVING, LOVING GOD LIVES THERE."

As the ringing of the bell at Holy Mass announces the coming of our Lord upon the altar, so the beatings of my heart are as sweet—low tinklings proclaiming He is within. . . . Not now and then, but all through the busy hours of the day and through the dreamings of the silences of night—my Lord is in my soul. Like our first parents in the garden, I am daily walking in the presence of my God, and my guardian angel ever close beside me is always looking within me, adoring and loving Him there.

Oh, it is wonderful! I shall never be frightened again when I am left alone, for alone is no more. . . . God is ever my silent guest . . . how sweet! . . . how merciful and consoling!

For His dear sake, what care I must take of my body—His temple. I must be free from every spot and stain of horrid sin. No careless looks, no evil words, no wicked acts. "Hands off, I am God's temple," I shall say. All girls and boys are His temples, too, and we must be just so. Like a faithful soldier, I must guard my temple well. If free from sin, it will be a house of purest gold.

And pearls? Where shall I gather them? I know. I know the pearls that He loves best. And not only a little circle shall He have but my temple must be covered everywhere with them. Kind acts, sweet thoughts—these are pearls. Cheerfully to help my tired mother; sweetly to give up to sister or brother the game or candy I so badly want; often to turn my thoughts within and softly whisper, "Dear God, I love You best;" "Dear God, stay with me always;" to forget myself; to think of Him and others. These are the pearls He loves so well and beginning right away, each day, I must put a new one in my locket.

Tower of Ivory, House of Gold,
Help me all-holy to be,

Sinless and faultless—a temple all-fair
For the dear God Who dwells in me.

How good You are, my God, and what wonderful things Your great love makes You think of! No more need I stretch out my thoughts in prayer way up to You in heaven, but like Mary and Joseph, I find You in the temple—my temple. Quietly closing my eyes, I can bow my head and gently look within me into Your dear face. . . . Look into Your face fairer and sweeter and more tender and loving even than my own dear mother's.

I love to have You there, and I love to say, "God is in my soul—I am the temple of God"—I want to sing this all day long.

Oh, dearest Lord and dearest Lover of me, can I ever think of anything else? Oh, help me to keep this temple sweet and pure. . . . Dear Father, I have said, "I Belong to God" and now with You living in my soul, can I not say, "My God Belongs To Me"?

(Close your eyes, dear child—dear little temple of God—and kneel at Jesus' feet, talk to Him, thank Him, love Him, and at the end of all, say the Our Father.)

This story, "The Theater Fire," is #406 in Rev. Lawrence G. Lovasik's booklet, *The Catechism in Stories: The Creed.*

A GIRL OF ELEVEN had once gone to a theater which usually showed very objectionable movies. Maybe she did not even realize this. A fire broke out in the theater. When the people smelled the smoke, there was a panic. Everybody rushed for the doors. Some of the people fell and blocked the doorways so that others behind them were trapped in the burning building.

The little girl, remembering the importance of making an act of perfect contrition in time of danger, climbed to the stage and yelled at the top of her voice: "O my God, I am heartily sorry for having offended You . . ." She went through the whole act of contrition. She reminded all the people who were there to do the same thing in their own hearts since there was no hope of getting out alive.

More than two hundred people were burned to death in this tragedy. Though their bodies were destroyed by the fire, the example of a brave little girl saved their souls from burning forever in the depths of hell, because many of them may have been in mortal sin.

The two stories that follow are from Fr. Lawrence G. Lovasik's *Catechism in Stories, Revised Edition,* Bruce Publishing Company, 1956, pages 229 and 242, respectively.

"The White Terrier"

A BOY HAD a little white terrier and looked after him carefully. One winter morning when the dog had just been bathed, brushed, and combed, the boy and his sister agreed that Prince looked really beautiful, perfectly white for once.

It had snowed all night, but now the sun was shining. They went across the fields to the village shop, and suddenly the boy said, "Why, look at Prince! He's dirty again already!"

"He really looks dirty," said his sister. Then she found out why. "He isn't that dirty. It's only seeing him against the fresh sparkling snow that makes him look that way."

Application: Sometimes you may have a very good opinion of yourself because you may not have examined your conscience well. The best way to examine your conscience before confession is to think of the commandments of God and of the Church. By asking yourself honestly how you have sinned with regard to them, you will see that your soul is not so clean and white as you think it is. The commandments are like the fresh sparkling snow. They show you how good you should be in the sight of God.

"Queen of Seven Swords"

BILLY HAD a beautiful picture of the Mother of Sorrows over his bed. It showed the Blessed Mother's heart pierced with seven swords. Billy used to look at the picture each evening as he said his prayers and would always add three Hail Marys to the Blessed Virgin.

But one day Billy committed a mortal sin of impurity. He was sorry for his sin and, without going to confession, was going to receive Holy Communion the next morning. That night as he prayed before the picture of the Mother of Sorrows, he was ashamed to look at her because his conscience bothered him. He heard a voice saying, "Billy, why don't you look at me?"

Billy looked up. It seemed as if the Blessed Mother were saying to him, "Billy, take this sword," and she painfully pulled one of the seven swords from her heart, and handed it to him. Then she said, "Stab me in the heart with it."

Billy was frightened. He said, "Blessed Mother, I could never do that. I would never stab you."

"But you will stab me in the heart, Billy, if you receive Holy Communion in mortal sin tomorrow. Don't you know that you will be committing a sacrilege by receiving my Son into a sinful heart? Mortal sin nailed Jesus to the cross, Billy, and I would rather have you stab me in the heart than that you should nail my Son to the cross by a sacrilege."

Billy cried out, "Blessed Mother, forgive me. I am sorry."

Billy made a very good confession and then received Jesus into his heart. That night as he said his prayers before the picture of the Mother of Sorrows, she seemed to smile at him because his heart was clean and pure again.

Application: Billy made an act of perfect contrition for his sin the night before he intended to go to Communion, but he knew that this was not enough. The next morning he went to confession as he promised the Blessed Mother, and confessed his mortal sin. Then he went to Holy Communion. This incident shows how terrible a sacrilege is, since it is like stabbing the Blessed Mother, because sin crucifies her Son.

The following story is excerpted from *Father Brennan's Favorite Stories* by Rev. Gerald Brennan, The Bruce Publishing Company, 1964, pages 71-73.

"The World's Greatest Book"

DID YOU EVER WONDER how many books there are in this world? Why, there are millions of books in this world. Books in libraries! Books in schools! Books in stores! Books in homes! There are all kinds of books— history books, geography books, spelling books, story books, picture books, and many other kinds of books. It seems as though this world is just filled with books.

Of course, some books are not very good. But there are many books that are very, very fine. I wonder whether any boy or girl knows which book is the best book in the world! Which book is the world's greatest book?

Well, boys and girls, the world's greatest book was written on two pieces of wood. The words of the book were written in blood. The pages of the book were fastened together by five nails. There was only one chapter in the book, and it told a sad story. Yet, that story was a story of love. Now, I suppose you are all wondering what the name of that book was! Would you like to know the name of the world's greatest book? Listen to this story!

The story is about a very holy priest, Father Francis. Father Francis was a very old man; he had been a priest for over fifty years! Well, Father Francis was taken sick, and for ten months he wasn't able to leave his bed. Every day he became weaker and weaker.

One day a friend went to visit the sick priest. After they had a visit, the friend said the rosary, and Father Francis answered the prayers. Then, when the rosary was finished, Father Francis made a strange request.

"Please," said the old priest to his friend, "bring me my book!"

The friend wondered at this strange request. He knew that Father Francis was too sick to read, yet he wanted to please the poor old man. So, the friend went to a desk, picked up a prayer-book, and handed the prayer-book to Father Francis.

Father Francis held the prayer-book for just a moment, and shook his head. Then he handed the prayer-book back.

"Bring me my book!" said the old priest a second time.

The friend was puzzled. "Maybe he wants his Mass book," thought the friend to himself.

The friend arose, went to a table, and there he found a small Mass book. He handed the Mass book to Father Francis, but the old priest pushed the book aside.

Father Francis closed his eyes. His voice was weak, but he repeated for the third and fourth time: "Bring me my book! Bring me my book!"

"Father Francis," said the kind friend, "you have many books. Which book do you want?"

The old priest didn't answer for a long time. Then, he barely whispered: "Bring me my book! Bring me my book!"

The old priest's friend didn't know what to do. He thought perhaps Father Francis was dreaming. Anyway, he noticed a crucifix hanging on the wall. The friend took the crucifix from the wall and placed it in the old priest's hands.

Father Francis held the crucifix tightly. He opened his eyes and stared at the crucifix for a long time. Then, tears ran down his cheeks and he whispered: "Thanks, my friend, for bringing my book! For years this crucifix has been my book. This crucifix is the world's greatest book!" Father Francis didn't say any more. Within three minutes, the priest was dead.

Yes, boys and girls, the crucifix is the world's greatest book. If you study that book well, you'll learn many things. If you study the crucifix, you'll know why Jesus hangs there. Why did Jesus suffer so much? Because of sin! Jesus hated sin, and Jesus knew that sin would keep you out of heaven. Jesus felt that by His death you would learn to hate sin, and thus you would save your soul.

Oh, I hope that each one of you will make the crucifix your greatest book. Study the crucifix! Look at it often! Think! I promise you that if you study the crucifix and think about the sufferings of Jesus, you'll learn to hate sin. That's what Jesus wants you to do—to hate sin.

There is something else that you'll know if you study the crucifix. You'll know how much Jesus loves you. Jesus loves you so much that He died for you. Now, how much do you love Jesus? When you commit sin, do you show Jesus that you love Him? No, you do not.

Boys and girls, at the foot of the Cross you'll learn many things. You'll learn to hate sin. You'll learn to love Christ. Remember, the crucifix is the world's greatest book!

———————

Two more of Sr. M. Josita's poems from her book *Sing a Song of Holy Things* follow. They are taken from pages 87 and 48, respectively.

"Pardon Me, Jesus"

Jesus, I've been naughty;
Now I come to say,
"Please forgive Your little child.
Make me good today."

I promise to do better
In every word and way.
Then pardon me, my Jesus,
Pardon me today.

"The Ten Commandments"

The first Commandment says that I
Should pray to God alone.
And love Him more than anything
I think, or see, or own.

The Second one commands us all
To bless the Holy Name,
Not speak It when we're angry,
Nor in fun—'twould be a shame.

The Third Commandment tells us all
To keep the Lord's day well,
To go to Mass, to do kind acts,
And other prayers to tell.

The Fourth reminds us all to love
Our parents and obey,
That God may bless us while on earth
In every little way.

The Fifth Commandment tells us
We must not kill anyone,
Nor harm a person any way,
No matter how it's done.

The Sixth and Ninth Commandments tell us
Always to be pure,
And then we'll all be happy
And will make our heaven sure.

The Seventh says we may not steal
From any one at all,
And if we borrow, give it back—
A crayon or a ball.

The Eighth Commandment warns that we
Should never tell a lie,
Nor say mean things of others,
Though they have made us cry.

And by the Tenth and last command
God wants us all to be
Happy with what we have and own,
Not wishing all we see.

And if we keep these ten commands
That God gave us on stone,
We show Him that we want to live
For Him—for Him alone.

The following prayer comes from *The Little Flower Prayer Book* as edited by Rev. Albert Dolan, Carmelite Press, 1926, page 77.

O Divine Spirit! Penetrate my soul with true horror and loathing of sin. Grant that I may be more exact in the fulfillment of all my duties, and strengthen me by Your grace, that I may not again yield to temptation. Amen.

Discussion Questions

1. How does the knowledge that you are a living temple of God help you to develop an even deeper hatred of sin?
2. What "pearls" can you gather to put in your locket each day?
3. How does it change your relationship with God when you truly accept and believe that He resides in you? How does accepting that you are a temple of God affect your prayer life?
4. What does "The Theater Fire" teach us about contrition and the need for frequent confession? What does it teach us about the "occasion of sin"?

5. Explain in your own words the lesson of the short story "The White Terrier."

6. How does the story "Queen of Seven Swords" show us how to be sorry for sin? Do you believe that your sins hurt Jesus? Our Blessed Mother? The Church?

7. Make sure that you have a crucifix—"The World's Greatest Book"—hanging in your bedroom. Kneel before it each night when you make your examination of conscience. For over two thousand years, the Church has encouraged the faithful to meditate (think about) on the Passion (suffering) and Death of Jesus. Why did Jesus die? Be sure to study this book each night—and lovingly kiss His feet in gratitude. (You may wish to memorize the poem, "Pardon Me, Jesus," and recite it before the crucifix each night after your examination of conscience.)

8. Discuss those things the commandments forbid and those they direct. Pick one that is difficult for you and examine yourself nightly on that commandment for one week. Then pick another one to work on for the next week.

Prayerfully read through Section V of "A Gospel Examination of Conscience" beginning on page 151. End this session with an Act of Contrition or a prayer of your own creation.

Lesson Six
On Bad Confession

YOU SEE, my dear boys and girls, that I say the same thing over and over again; and I do it because at your young age, unless you hear a thing more than once, there is danger that you will let it drop from your minds entirely. This last would be a very great evil in things which are necessary or useful for making you good children, first, and afterwards good men and good women. There are some things which are not so necessary and if you forget them, it really does not make much—if any—difference. There are other things which you must always remember. A great deal of harm might happen to you if you lost sight of them.

I think that somewhere in your catechism, the question is asked, "What are the four last things to be remembered?" Some children think that the question refers to the four things we are to remember last, as if they were four things that we need not think of until we have thought of everything else. But the question means, "What are the four last things which we must never forget?"

Now, as you know, these things are: Death, judgment, heaven, and hell. They are the four things which must happen last to every man. They must not be lost sight of. When one stops remembering—that is thinking—that he is going to die, that he is going to be judged, that there is a hell for him to escape and a heaven for him to win, there is great danger that he will not be on his guard, that he will be overtaken by sin and that he will die before he has been sorry or pardoned for his sin and thus will be lost forever. The only way for one not to forget these things is to hear about them often.

So, to come back to what I began with, you understand why I tell you so often the same thing. It may tire you, but I do not wish you to forget.

In this instruction, we will try to understand what it is to make a bad confession. Do you know, my dear children, any words that look as wicked as the words "bad confession?" Are they not words that frighten you? Do they not seem to mean something awful, something terrible? That is the way they look and sound to me. There are other words also which when they are spoken make one shudder. These are the words "bad"—or that which is the same thing—"sacrilegious Communion." Then there is another word which is worse than either of the words we have been thinking of. That word is "Depart from me." It is what Christ is going to say on Judgment Day—on the last day—to those whom, on account of their sins, He cannot admit to heaven and whom He must drive away from Him and send to hell, where they will not look on His beautiful face forever. Now in a way these three words are almost the same. Why? Because a bad confession leads to a bad Communion and a bad Communion is such a great sin, so heinous—that is, so insulting—to God's sanctity and to God's grace, that it is certainly opening the door that looks out on the path that leads to hell.

When the Devil beholds anyone going to Communion knowingly in the state of sin, he begins to feel that sooner or later that guilty one will fall into the dark and dreary and wretched and pitiless empire of which he is the ruler.

I have asked you during these days to pray for many things, but I beg you to pray most earnestly never to make a bad confession or Communion. I have asked you to make many resolutions, but I beseech you, let your strongest resolution be rather to die than commit the sin of a bad confession or a bad Communion. You must know that you make a bad confession when you hide willingly a sin that you are obliged to tell.

Here I will ask you a question. What sins must you tell in confession in order that your confession may be as it should be? You must tell in confession all your mortal sins. Does the law make it necessary for you to reveal to the priest any other of your sins? No. Understand that in confession you need tell your mortal sins alone. Less grievous faults you are not called upon to make known. However, let me give this piece of advice. Get into the habit of making all your sins known. It will bring you more grace, that is, you will find that God will come more quickly to your help. His blessings will be more numerous. Besides, it will prove that you wish to have nothing at all to do with sin, be it small or great, which is the best frame of mind for you to be in when you approach the Sacrament of Penance. Still I must put things to you as they are. Unless you willfully—that is, knowing what you are doing—keep back a mortal sin your confession is not bad. I say your confession is not bad if you are really sorry, that is, sorry in the way I have been explaining to you all along, for the sins you have told.

> A bad confession is when you hide willingly a sin that you are obliged to tell.

Now there are more ways than one of making a bad confession. Do you know that there are no two words joined together that seem to me to have a more shocking sound than those two I have been using so much in this instruction—"bad confession." Yes, there are another couple of words which have a more fearful sound. I mean the two words "bad Communion." When we think what a beautiful thing confession is, and what a grand thing Communion is, we easily understand that to make either of them a bad thing must mean a great accident for the one who is guilty enough to do so.

If you are not sorry for your sins when you tell them to the priest in confession, if you are not grieved for every one of them without exception, then your confession is worth nothing. I am speaking, as you know, of mortal sins. You will remember what I have said about sorrow, or about contrition, which is the same thing. You are not obliged to feel it as you would some hurt or some pain. The best proof that you are really sorry is that you really wish that you had not done any of the things you are making known to your confessor, that you wish this not because somebody—your friends or your parents—has found you out, or because some other damage has happened to you, something you do not like or something that makes you uneasy, but you wish the fault had never been yours because it put you in danger of being lost forever, because it put you in danger of never reaching heaven, or because it displeased God. These three reasons for being sorry make up a very good act of contrition.

> The best proof that you are sorry is that you wish you had not done those things.

Another proof of a real worthy contrition is that you have made up your mind that never—however much you may be tempted—never will you offend God again. Suppose you told, let me say, ten sins in confession and you meant never to do those wrong things again—all ten of them—then you are all right. But suppose you said to yourself: I will not commit nine of those sins any more, but there is the tenth and I have been guilty of it so often that I intend to do it all over again, then your confession would be a bad one, and though you were really sorry for the nine others you are not forgiven any one of them because you have no contrition for that awful tenth mortal sin, whatever it may be.

Why will not God forgive you the nine others? I will try to explain this to you. Sin is a thought or a word or an act which offends God. Sin is a sin only because it offends God and makes the sinner an enemy of God. Suppose you have committed ten sins and you are sorry for nine only, the tenth sin still keeps you an enemy of God—not only keeps you an enemy, but of your own free will, by that sin for which you have no regret and which you mean to be guilty of again when you have the temptation or a chance, you wish to continue as an enemy of God. You see that by this act of yours you simply say to the Lord that you do not wish to be His friend. How can He, when you behave like this, forgive any of your faults? It is not hard for you to understand that if you have not real sorrow for every one of your sins your confession is worth nothing—is a bad confession.

Another reason why a confession may be bad is because the boy or girl does not tell the priest every sin. If this happens because you forget, then it is not a bad confession. But if this happens because you are afraid or ashamed, if through shame or fear you hold back a mortal sin, then your confession is a bad confession. Always remember that your confession in this case cannot be bad unless the sin you hide is a mortal sin. I will repeat that in confession the only sins you must tell are your mortal ones.

> Sin is a sin only because it offends God and makes the sinner an enemy of God.

What about your venial sins? Must you tell them to your confessor? No, you are not obliged in conscience to do so. Is it well to do so? Yes, indeed it is. Another time I will explain to you how you may get rid of venial sins without going to confession, but let me say just now the surest way to receive pardon for them is to tell them in the Sacrament of Penance and get absolution for them.

For the most part children, and older people, make bad confessions because they are either ashamed or afraid to tell certain sins by which they have broken the law of God. Now, my dear children, what is it that makes you afraid? Do you stand in fear of the priest? If so, why? He is not going to harm you in any way. You say,

> Most people make bad confessions because they are ashamed or afraid to tell certain sins.

but if I tell him that, he is going to give me an awful scolding. First, the priest does not always scold; secondly, there are some priests who never scold. You must remember that you are always free to choose whatever confessor you please. You are never obliged to go to any one priest. This you must never forget. You all have your "likes and dislikes." It is only natural. Therefore, make your confession to whatsoever priest you please. If you think that such a Father is easier than another, go to the one who is the easier of the two.

Now, let me suppose that the priest is going to scold you on account of the sins or some special sin that you committed and which you must tell him. Suppose he is going to give you a very severe scolding. Let me ask you, do you not deserve it? You know that were you to die in the state of mortal sin, you would be lost forever. Now what is a scolding compared with an eternity of suffering? Eternity never ends, and this scolding you are so much in dread of will be gone and forgotten in a very short time. Not only it will pass as all things pass, but it will, I am sure, do you much good. The greatest good it can do you is to make you sorry for your sins and perhaps it may prevent you from ever falling into that sin again. Now what is a scolding? It is finding fault with you in harsh words and in severe tones. That is all. You may feel it very much. So much the better. Anything is preferable to having God angry with you and obliged to tell you to go away from Him forever.

So, my dear children, be sensible. If you are going to be scolded, as you call it, if the priest is very angry, bear with it and take it all as a little bit of penance for the sins of which you may be guilty. You will always find that the greater your sins are, the gladder the priest will be to see you in confession and the kinder will be his treatment of you. You must always bear in mind that the priest in the confessional is there in the place of Christ and has all Christ's power. You may be sure that he will always welcome you, that he will remember how Christ, whose place he holds, has been impatient to have you come and in a humble way tell your sins and have them forgiven.

Yes, Christ has been waiting for you to come to Him and be His friend again, and have your souls made white and go and sin no more. Drive, therefore, out of your head the thought that the priest is going to be hard with you. He will talk seriously to you, he will advise you and caution you and tell you what you must do not to fall into those wrong doings in the days to come.

So you see, you must go into the confessional without any fear. You must look upon the confessor as your best friend. He has no wish to hurt you. His only desire is to make you hate all that is bad and love all that is good. He has only one thing in view and that is to fill your souls with the love of God and to make you fear more than anything else to offend God, and to make you more afraid to commit sin than

> Christ has been waiting for you to come to Him.

to have the worst thing, even death itself, happen to you. Knowing all this, what is there that should make you dread going to confession? On the contrary, is there not everything to make you happy and thank God for having the chance to wipe out every wrong thought, wrong word, wrong act and then to look up into the face of your Lord and see not a frown, but only the sweetest of all smiles to show you how pleased He is to have you once more as His child whom He loves and who loves Him?

There is another cause, as I told you already in this instruction, there is another cause of bad confessions. That cause is shame. You are ashamed to let the priest know that you have been guilty of this or that sin. I made little of the fear that some have of confessing their sins. I make just as little of your being ashamed. You are ashamed of the priest; you blush because of the priest. You say to yourself: What will the priest think of me? He is going to think poorly of me; he is going to have a bad, a low opinion of me.

He is not going to do anything of the kind. He knows how strong the Devil is and how weak you are. He is sure that there is nothing too shameful for a poor child to do when that child forgets God and does not ask Him for help. And you never think of God knowing all your thoughts? You never think that you cannot conceal anything from Him? You are ashamed of the priest who after all is only a man, and you are not ashamed of God? This is really a big mistake. Why were you not ashamed in the beginning to commit this sin which you do not wish the priest to hear? Be not ashamed to lay open your conscience to the confessor. The shame you feel will be part of your penance.

If there is any guilt of yours which you think you cannot bear to confess, the best thing to do is to tell the priest that there is another sin or other sins you have not the courage to tell. He will understand. He will put to you a few questions and in a minute the whole trouble will be over. Do not leave the church today without promising to God that no matter what you may do you will not hide a sin in confession.

Thus all your confessions will be good ones and you will grow better and better every day of your lives.

Discussion Questions

1. What are the last four things upon which we should meditate?
2. What is a bad confession? Why is it such a danger?
3. What three reasons for being sorry make up a very good act of contrition?
4. What kind of sins are we always obliged to confess to a priest?
5. What are the two main reasons that people make bad confessions? How can you overcome this?
6. How does the knowledge that Jesus, in the form of the priest, is waiting for you in the confessional help relieve some of the fear of confessing your sins?
7. Discuss the following: "Be not ashamed to lay open your conscience to the confessor. The shame you feel will be part of your penance."

I Talk with God

Dear Jesus, I am going to confession. I am going to tell my sins to the priest. He will make the Sign of the Cross over me. This means that You, Jesus, forgive my sins. The Sign of the Cross reminds me that You died because of my sins. It also reminds me that You are hurt by sin. You suffered on the Cross. Dear Jesus, I am sorry I have sinned. Help me to make a good confession. (Prayer by Sister M. Imelda)

OR

O my God, help me to make a good confession. Mary, my dearest mother, pray to Jesus for me. My holy Angel Guardian, my Patron Saint [name], pray for me. Help me to examine my conscience, enable me to obtain true sorrow for my sins, and beg for me the grace rather to die than to offend God again. (From *The Little Flower Prayer Book,* Carmelite Press, 1926)

For older children and adults: Fr. Halpin explains that we may be forgiven our venial sins in ways other than going to confession—although there are many graces to be obtained by doing so. The *Catechism of the Catholic Church* cites several methods of forgiveness for venial sins: ". . . Through the Eucharist those who live from the life of Christ are fed and strengthened. 'It is a remedy to free us from our daily faults and to preserve us from mortal sins.' Reading Sacred Scripture, praying the Liturgy of the Hours and the Our Father—every sincere act of worship or devotion revives the spirit of conversion and repentance within us and contributes to the forgiveness of our sins" (Nos. 1436-1437).

"Prayer for Daily Neglects"

Eternal Father, I offer Thee the Sacred Heart of Jesus, with all its love, all its sufferings and all its merits. First —To expiate [make up for] all the sins I have committed this day and during all my life. Gloria Be to the Father . . .

Second—To purify the good I have done poorly this day and during all my life. Gloria Be to the Father . . .

Third—To supply for the good I ought to have done, and that I have neglected this day and all my life. Gloria Be to the Father . . . Amen.

(A Poor Clare nun, who just died, appeared to her abbess who was praying for her, and said to her: "I went straight to heaven, for, by means of this prayer, recited every evening, I paid all my debts.")

Lesson Six Read-aloud Stories and Poem

This story, "You Do Some Choosing (Hell)," is from *I Belong to God, Great Truths in Simple Stories for Children and Lovers of Children* by Lillian Clark, Longmans, Green and Company, 1936, pages 43-52.

HELL! GOODNESS, is not that a swear word and is it not sinful to say it? No, not always. It is sinful only when angry men use it to mean something wicked. Oftentimes to say it is bad manners, but it is quite right to use it as we do today and speak of it as we speak of places and countries. In your geography, you study about Canada and Europe and hear of people visiting them, and just so we may study about hell, but—there is no visiting there. Alas! People who journey to hell stay on forever.

A gentleman last May decided to buy a new summer home to take his family into the country for the whole vacation time. The children were all excited. "Oh goody," they said, "Where is it to be, Daddy?" "Either Rosedale or Highland," he answered, "I cannot tell which until I find out something more about each place—what kind of scenery, fishing, swimming, what sort of people, and what they do all day."

Now, child, you know that at the end of your life you, too, are going off into a new country, and like the gentleman you must choose between two places, and like him also you should spend some time in finding out about each. And, how important it is, for when you go you are to stay, not three or four months only, but for millions and millions of years, that is—forever.

"Oh," you answer, "I know what you mean. You mean I am to choose between heaven and hell. That is very

113

easy. I do not need to think about that a minute, for who would ever choose hell?" No one, of course. No, no one ever really means to choose hell, and yet how is it there are people there? Maybe we can find our answer in this remark of a little six-year-old. She said one day: "I am sure there are more people in hell than in heaven." "Why, Helen?" she was asked. "Because—because bad is easier than good." And so it is. To keep, therefore, from doing the bad, which is very easy, and to force ourselves to do the good, even when it is hard, we should have deep down in our minds a clear picture of fearful, frightful, awful hell, and we should look at it when we find ourselves slipping and almost giving in.

Today, then, we shall study hell—and I think a story of a real and true boy named Georgie will help us. He was a brown-eyed, rosy-cheeked little fellow of two summers and he lived a few steps away from a convent chapel. Each evening as the shadows began to fall and bedtime drew near, his mother brought him there to say his little prayers and it was sweet to see the tiny mite not stopping till at the tabernacle, close to his Jesus, he would lisp a loving goodnight. Then, turning each time, the baby feet would patter softly to our Lady's altar for a second goodnight, and to ask the care and love of his dear Mother Mary.

With Christmas, of course, came the little manger and its precious Infant, and then the visits grew longer and his mother must hold him close to the little crib. Bending near he would softly call "Babee" and "Jesus" and say funny little words besides—sweetest words that only babies know—and which I am very sure the Christ Child understood.

After his mother he would repeat—

Were I to hold You, Baby-God
I'd whisper in Your ear
How much I love You—then some things,
For only You to hear.

Then would come a loving goodnight kiss right on the dear Infant's curls and little Georgie would go away sweetly, crowing with joy.

One by one the holidays slipped by and he came, impatient as ever, his eager baby feet hurrying to the crib, running on ahead of his mother, calling, "Babee-Babee." But lo, at last Christmas time was over and the little manger was gone. This evening he looked— he stopped— he looked again. He was puzzled. "Babee" he called. . . . "Babee," again and again, and then down, down on hands and knees searching with wide, round, wondering eyes—searching everywhere—ceiling, floor and walls. Rising slowly "Babee," and "gone" he whispered plaintively. His eyes, like twin moons in a sky of pale rose, clouded with sudden pain, and Mother quickly folding him in her arms, carried him off, as little sobs and big round tears and smothered cries told how he missed his little Friend.

SEVERAL YEARS PASS—

Our little man is now a boy of six. It is the year of his First Holy Communion and every Sunday brings him with loving heart and shining eyes to receive his well-loved Jesus. We see him as before coming daily to the chapel for his goodnight prayer.

Good Friday comes, and let us watch them this evening as they walk silently in and with soft step pass towards the tabernacle. The quick, loving eyes of the child tell him at once something is missing. "Mamma, the little light is out," he whispers. "Yes, dear," his mother says, and drawing him closer goes on with her prayers. How strange that Mamma does not seem disturbed, he thinks—I guess she did not hear me. "Mamma, the little light is out," he says again, "and "Oh, Mamma, the little door is open." "Yes, dear, Jesus is not there." "Not there, Mamma?" he says with a little quiver looking towards the altar. "No, my little son, this is the day bad, wicked men took Jesus off and killed Him." An ache springs into the child's heart, and pain flashes into his eyes as he searches his mother's face, then bursting into sobs, he buries his head in the deep fur of her coat. Just as in his baby days, he is taken out sobbing and weeping. Try as she can, his mother fails to comfort him, and it is only sleep that ends his flood of tears. But his heartache is not ended, and often through the night little sighs and troubled words escape his lips just as before, and "Babee"; and "gone"; and "No Jesus Sunday" they hear him say.

Now, little reader, did you never miss Jesus like that on Good Friday? Did you never think that on that day in all the churches the world over, the little red lights are out and the little tabernacle doors are open and the Jesus Whom you love to have on the altar is gone? No? Well, think of it now for a while. . . . Imagine this to be Good Friday and think that you are where you love to go to Holy Mass on Sunday, or in the convent chapel where you sometimes go for visits. . . . Pretend that the little light is out and the door open, telling you Jesus is not there. . . . Then let your mind travel from city to city, and from church to church in every country without finding one red light burning and seeing all the little open doors telling their sad story that Jesus is gone.

[Keep this picture in your mind and stop reading and close your eyes and think deeply of it.]

Would not the Church be very cold and cheerless without Jesus? Does not your heart grow sad at the thought of a world without Him even for a day? Would you not ache all over and would not such a feeling of loneliness steal into your heart that you would hurry home to Mother for comfort and a warm embrace? Could you be happy and smile again until the priest had brought the dear Lord back in Holy Mass tomorrow?

But suppose something should keep the priest from saying Mass the next day and the next and the next—how distressed and anxious you would become. And then if right away cruel war should carry off our priests and kill them all and none should be left to say the precious words to change the bread and wine—what would you do? Why you would weep and sigh and pine and almost die of grief, and forgetting all else you would call upon God to take you quickly from this chilly world; to take you away to heaven to be again near Jesus. You would hurry by the churches, now so cold and empty . . . and you would meet sad faces and breaking hearts at every turn, and earth would be a gloomy place. . . .

[Stop reading again and with closed eyes go over that picture.]

Now do some more supposing. Suppose from grieving and weeping like little George you should fall sobbing asleep. And in a dream should see one of God's beautiful angels passing over the troubled world as the angels did on the first Christmas night, but instead of a song of joy you should hear him saying, "Wicked world, because of your sins Jesus has left your altars, but think not to meet Him in heaven, for I have come from God with this message—'Heaven is closed as a book folded up and for you it shall never be opened.'" Oh! how you would moan and toss in your sleep. How dark and fearful this thought would be—never to go to heaven, never to see the smile of God, never to see the sweet face of the Virgin Mother; but instead to hear the demons of hell shrieking bad words into your ears and laughing at you, right into your face for believing their lies and letting them draw you into that GODLESS place.

[With your eyes closed think earnestly, child, of hell as it really is until you are sure as sure can be that you will never, never choose it.]

Then say, "My God and dearest Father, give me that love of You and great desire for You; and give me also that understanding and fear of hell that will keep me always in Your grace."

[Say all that is in your heart about it to Jesus, dear child; He is listening. Then end by praying a loving Our Father.]

———

The next two short stories are again from Fr. Lawrence G. Lovasik's booklet, *Catechism in Stories: The Creed,* Nos. 410 and 412, respectively.

"St. Joan's Confession"

JOAN OF ARC, the maid of France, was subjected to a severe religious and theological examination during her trial. One of her examiners asked, "Do you believe that you shall surely be saved?"

"Yes, I firmly believe that I shall surely be saved." Since Joan was known to have gone to confession almost every day, the inquisitors then inquired of her, "If you believe that you shall be saved, what, then, is the need of your going to confession so often?"

Joan then made this reply, *"My soul can never be made too clean."*

"The Ambassador of Christ"

A NON-CATHOLIC FRIEND of a priest voiced his opinion about confession. "I believe that God alone can forgive sins, and you priests are not divine. You are human like us all and make mistakes and have your faults and weaknesses. You have no more power to forgive sins than anyone else."

"Can you give a man in the Sing Sing prison a pardon just the same as the governor?" the priest asked.

"No, I can't do that."

"But you are a man, just as he is. Didn't you say that you had as much power to forgive a misdeed as any other man?"

"Yes," replied the non-Catholic, "but I make a distinction. The governor simply as a man does not have that power to pardon. It is only because of his office as governor that he has such authority."

"Then you admit." said the priest, "that same basic distinction which the Church makes: the distinction between a priest and any other human being is that a priest is one who exercises the office of an ambassador. He has been given the power to forgive sins by Christ Himself."

The following short story, "The Joy of a Good Confession," comes from *Children's Retreats* by Rev. P.A. Halpin, 1926, page 170.

IT IS TOLD that a certain man had committed a great crime, and although his mind was filled with remorse, and although he was most unhappy, he could not make up his mind to go to confession. He saw hell open beneath his feet, and he could neither eat nor sleep.

When he had lived in this sad condition for about ten years, he met on a journey a priest, with whom he entered into conversation. One of the things of which the priest spoke was the happiness that follows a good confession, and how grateful we should be to Jesus Christ for giving us so easy a means of living a happy life.

The man, on hearing these words, showed by his troubled countenance that he was unhappy. The priest said to him: "My friend, perhaps my words have grieved you, or have brought to your mind some sad remembrance."

"Yes," he replied, "I am indeed unhappy."

The priest spoke to him with the utmost kindness, and soon learned the cause of his trouble. "Come with me," he said, "I will soon remove from you that heavy weight that oppresses you." Saying this, he led him to the nearest church, and made him go to confession.

As soon as he had received absolution, he came out of the confessional, and leaped and ran about as one who had suddenly become demented.

"What is the matter?" asked the priest in alarm.

The repentant sinner answered, "It seems to me that I could almost fly up to heaven, for I feel so free and happy. During the last ten years, I lived as if I had been already in hell. But at this moment I feel as if I were in heaven, I am so happy."

———

This story, "Don't Be a Monkey," is excerpted from Father Brennan's book, *Angel City,* published by The Bruce Publishing Company, 1948, pages 31-34.

. . . THIS IS A STORY about a man who sold hats. They were baseball hats, the kind boys wear when they play baseball.

It was a very warm day and the man went from store to store, trying to sell his hats. But I guess that nobody wanted to buy hats that day. Luck was bad. The man was tired, very tired, and so, he went out into the country. There he found a nice big apple tree. He lay down on the ground and fell asleep.

For two hours he slept, and then he awoke. He rose up and picked up his suitcase. It seemed very light. He opened it, and what do you think? The suitcase was empty. All of his little hats were gone. Someone had stolen his little hats. And was he mad!

Then all of a sudden, he heard a noise. He looked up into the tree, and what do you think he saw? The tree was full of monkeys, and on the head of each little monkey was one of the man's little hats. The hat man scratched his head, wondering what he could do, and right away, all of the little monkeys scratched their heads.

Then the man yelled, and right after him all of the monkeys yelled. The man stamped his foot, and sure enough, all of the monkeys stamped their feet. The man waved his arms, and all of the monkeys waved their arms. Then the man walked up and down, and so did the monkeys walk up and down. By this time, the man was awfully mad. He was so mad that he pulled his own hat off his head and threw the hat down on the ground.

And what do you think happened? Why, all of the monkeys took the hats which they had stolen from the poor man, and threw them down on the ground at his feet. So the man recovered his hats.

I told that story because I think that it has a lesson for all of us. Don't be a monkey! You know monkeys always do whatever they see someone else do. That's just what the monkeys did in this story. And that's just what some boys and girls do. They make monkeys out of themselves. They do just what some other boys and girls do. But the sad part is that they always do what the bad boys and girls do.

If the girl next door sasses her mother, then you want to do the same thing. You make a monkey of yourself. If you see some little boy steal, then you steal too. You make a monkey out of yourself. If your friends swear, then you swear. If your friends laugh and talk in church, you laugh and talk in church. If your friends stay away from confession and Holy Communion, you do the same thing. If your friends miss Mass, you miss Mass. You make a monkey out of yourself!

Whenever we make sins, we make monkeys out of ourselves: we do just what the Devil does. You know the Devil is always trying to make a monkey out of us. He has lots of time on his hands, and he spends all of his time showing boys and girls how to be bad, how to make sins, how to go to hell. Whenever you sin, you follow the Devil. You do just what he shows you to do. Let's not make monkeys out of ourselves. Don't let the Devil make a monkey out of you!

That was my advice to the children of Angel City. And to the little boy or girl who is reading this page, I say: "Don't let the Devil make a monkey out of you."

The following poem, "Take Care," is from *Religious Poems for Little Folks*, The Bruce Publishing Company, 1936, pages 123-124.

Little children, you must seek
Rather to be good than wise,
For the thoughts you do not speak
Shine out in your cheeks and eyes.

If you think that you can be
Cross or cruel, and look fair,
Let me tell you how to see
You are quite mistaken there.

Go and stand before the glass,
And some ugly thought contrive,
And my word will come to pass
Just as sure as you're alive!

What you have, and what you lack,
All the same as what you wear,
You will see reflected back;
So, my little folks, take care!

And not only in the glass
Will your secrets come to view;
All beholders, as they pass,
Will perceive and know them too.

Goodness shows in blushes bright,
Or in eyelids dropping down,
Like a violet from the light;
Badness, in a sneer or frown.

Out of sight, my boys and girls,
Every root of beauty starts;
So think less about your curls,
More about your minds and hearts.

Cherish what is good, and drive
Evil thoughts and feelings far;
For, as sure as you're alive,
You will show for what you are.
—Alice Cary

Discussion Questions

1. When we think about hell, sometimes it is hard to imagine what it is really like. The story "You Do Some Choosing" helps us view hell as a place without Jesus—a place with no goodness, no peace, no love—no one to watch over and care for us. In your own words, describe how this story has helped you to hate sin.
2. What do you think of St. Joan's statement, "My soul can never be made too clean"?
3. Other than the power to forgive sins, discuss what other powers Christ has given to our beloved priests.
4. Describe in your own words why the man in "The Joy of a Good Confession" was so happy.
5. When have you been a "monkey"? What can you do to stop this behavior?
6. In her poem, what does Alice Cary mean when she says, "You will show for what you are"? Have you ever tried to hide an angry thought? What lesson do you think this poem is trying to teach?

Prayerfully read through Section VI of "A Gospel Examination of Conscience" beginning on page 152. End this session with an Act of Contrition or a prayer of your own creation.

Lesson Seven
Satisfaction

WE HAVE COME to the last instruction of this retreat which you have been making in order to prepare yourselves for receiving all the blessings of the great Sacrament of Penance. During these talks of mine, I have simply explained every word of the definition which you find in your catechism and which you have learned by heart. I told you that it was a sacrament and therefore instituted by Christ. He gave us this sacrament so that whenever we fell into sin after baptism we could get cleansed from that sin and once more enjoy His friendship. It is called the Sacrament of Penance because the word "penance" means pain or sorrow for having offended God. I told you that sin was the willful breaking of the law of God. I tried to make you understand that sin is the worst evil that can happen to you here on this earth. I spoke of the different kinds of sin—of original, of actual, of mortal and of venial sin. We talked of the kind of sorrow that we should have for all our sins. It was not any kind of sorrow, but a grief for sin because it either put you in danger of never seeing God or—which is better—because you have offended God whom you wish to love above everybody and everything else.

If you are prepared when you go to confession, that is, if you tell all your sins of thought, or word, or deed and tell them with the sorrow of which I have just spoken to you, then your sins will be forgiven. In other words, if you do not make a bad confession (and you know now when a confession is bad), then as soon as the priest gives you absolution all your faults are wiped out and it depends entirely on you never to sin again and always to walk in the sunshine of God's love, which is something worth more than anything, or all things, in this world.

In all my talks to you, what have I done? I have only taken what you find in your catechism as the definition of this sacrament for which you are getting ready, and told you as fully as I could the meaning of each word. I would like to say right here that there is one thing you must pay attention to, not only now, but during all the time you go to religion classes. That one thing is: Always learn your catechism lesson so well by heart that it will be impossible for anyone to make you stumble while you recite it. It may be that sometimes you will not understand the meaning of some of the words. Never mind, for as you grow older the meaning of these things will be clear and not only you will know what you should believe and do, but also you will be able to tell others what the right thing is and in the proper words.

I am sure you will always be able to put in the correct language for yourselves and others what the Church calls the Sacrament of Penance. You will know that it is a sacrament, but it has certain signs which anybody can see—signs that show what it does for your souls.

Sin is the willful breaking of the law of God.

The one who goes to confession gives a sign that he has turned away from sin, and the priest by his words and actions gives us to understand that he is with the power given him by God, through Christ, pardoning the sins which are told him by the sinner who is sorry for his sins.

In your catechism there are seven sacraments, four of which are ordinarily received by youth: Baptism, Penance, Confirmation, Holy Eucharist. About these two last sacraments you will hear a good deal when you advance to the class of those who are preparing to receive those two great sacraments. These sacraments are entirely different, the one from the other, but they are like each other in that they were instituted by Christ and they give grace to our souls.

Baptism and Confirmation are alike in that neither of them can be received more than once. You cannot be baptized or confirmed twice. But you may go to confession and Communion frequently.

How often should you go to confession? It is best to follow in this the regulations of your parish and I think that according to them the pastor calls all his children who have not made their first Communion to go to confession at least four times a year, generally during the Ember Days[9]. If you want a rule for your whole life, I would say the more often you go, the better. You remember that there is no limit to the mercy of God. Peter once asked our Lord if sin might be forgiven seven times and our Lord answered: ". . . I say to you, not seven times but seventy-seven times."[10] I would ask you to go to confession as soon as possible in case you fall into mortal sin. It is very dangerous to remain even a few seconds in that state. Suppose you were to die with that sin on your soul; what would become of you? Your faith teaches you that you would be lost forever. You know how uncertain life is. It does not take a second to die, and you might drop dead at any moment. Boys and girls think that sudden deaths happen to grown people only. Many, many children have died suddenly.

Sometimes it may be impossible for you to get to the priest. The church may be far away or there may

The more often you go to confession, the better.

[9] Prior to 1969, three consecutive days of fasting and abstinence were honored at the beginning of each season, including the Wednesday, Friday, and Saturday that follow December 13, the first Sunday of Lent, Pentecost, and September 14.
[10] Matthew 18:22

be other reasons. If you have to wait days, or, as some-times happens, weeks and even months before you can go to confession, there is one way to protect yourself against the awful fate of being with the damned forev-er. That one way is to make as hearty an act of contri-tion as it is in your power to make. I told you of one kind of contrition which is so powerful that by it, even with-out confession, you will be forgiven your sin. Do your best to make such an act and with prayer you will suc-ceed in doing so.

You see, I have come again to talk of sin and immed-iately I think of the awful evils it brings about. The only thing that can surely save you from it is confession fre-quently and properly made, and after confession comes prayer and that form of prayer especially that is called the "Act of Contrition." As I have told you there is a cer-tain act of contrition which—joined with confession—will get you pardon from your sins—that contrition is called attrition.

St. Alphonsus, who was the founder of the great Re-demptorist order, puts in the following words that kind of contrition of which I have just been speaking and that I might call an "Act of Attrition": *"My God, because by my sins I have lost heaven and deserved hell for eter-nity, I am sorry above all things for having offended You and, I firmly purpose never more to offend You by a mortal sin."* These words show that you are really sorry for sin, but only for the reason that your sin might be and could have been the cause of everlasting injury to you. Such an act made in confession would have been enough to rid you of all the sins you told to the priest. Without—that is, outside of the sacrament—it would have been of little benefit to you.

There is another Act of Contrition. If you make it sin-cerely, that is, from the bottom of your heart, even out-side of confession, it will gain for you the pardon of all your sins. It is certainly worthwhile to learn to make this act, for it is so pleasing in the eyes of God that were you to die after it you could not be lost; you would find yourselves in presence of your judge without a mortal sin on your soul and so the sentence that He would pronounce would be altogether in your favor. This Act of Contrition which, when made honestly and meaning every word of it, can do so much for your soul, even outside of confession, I will give you also in the words of St. Alphonsus Liguori.

You remember that I said the saints always made this perfect act of sorrow, at least they were ever striving to make it and were ever praying for the grace to make it. We learn that St. Margaret of Cortona spent the remainder of her life, after her conversion, shedding tears of such real grief for her sins that it was told her by a messenger from heaven that God was "so touched by her sorrow that every one of her faults, no matter how grievous they had been, was so entirely blotted out that her soul had become as white as it was the day she was baptized." Yes, the saints so understood the value of this great grace, that they preferred to make one such Act of Contrition, rather than be made masters of the whole world. This is the act as made by St. Alphonsus: *"My God, because You are infinitely good, I love You above all things, and because I love You, I am sorry above all things for the offenses I have committed against You, O Sovereign Good. My God, I resolve never more to offend You. I wish to die rather than offend You again by mortal sin."*

You see all that is meant in that Act of Contrition. It is not necessary to use the words I have just repeated. Any words meaning the same thing will do as well. It is very useful to have some fixed set of words. The words that you find in your catechism are just as good as the words of the saint. I wished simply to put before you the way which a saint thinks is the right way to make this wonderful act of sorrow. I would beg of you to try to make this act any time you may have—which God forbid—the misfortune to commit a grievous sin. I advise you to make it every night before you go to bed. I advise you to make it in moments of danger and I know God will give you the grace to make it on your deathbed. It must not be forgotten that when you make this act in the state of mortal sin, *you must have the desire and the intention of going to confession as soon as you can.*

Your catechism says that the Sacrament of Penance is made up of three parts: confession, contrition and satisfaction[11]. I must say a few words about satisfaction. Satisfaction means that which the penitent—the one who goes to confession—must do himself, in order to make up to God for his sins. This "making up" is necessary. Hence the priest obliges you, when you have confessed, to say some prayers or to do something as penance for your sins. When sins are forgiven, there is no longer any eternal punishment to be suffered, but there remains something for the sinner to endure. The enduring of that something is called satisfaction or penance.

So you must, when you have told all your sins, pay attention to every word the priest says. He will tell you how you will be able to avoid those sins of yours in the future, he will give you some advice, and, above all, he

---

[11] The *Compendium of Catechism of the Catholic Church* lists two essential elements: Acts of the penitent (a careful *examination of conscience*; *contrition* [perfect or imperfect]; *confession* [the telling of one's sins to the priest]; and *satisfaction* [the carrying out of certain acts of penance which the confessor imposes upon the penitent to repair the damage caused by sin]) and absolution of the priest (Nos. 302-303).

will give you some penance to perform. Do not miss a word your confessor says. He is speaking to you in the name of the Great High Priest Jesus Christ, and his words will do you very much good. Above all, be sure you understand what he tells you to do for penance or what he tells you to say. If you are not sure, do not hesitate to ask him to please repeat it for you. Be very childlike with your confessor in all things and in this matter of penance as well as in everything else.

> Do not miss a word your confessor says.

Lest I forget it, I will mention here something that it is very necessary for you to know and remember. In the beginning of our retreat, or perhaps a little later, I gave you the reasons why you should never yield to the temptation to hide a sin in confession. I explained to you that if the penitent willfully neglects to mention a sin or sins which should be confessed, or tells a lie about any serious sin, he not only does not obtain the pardon of his sins, but makes himself guilty of a greater sin— he makes himself guilty of a bad confession. In other words, he commits a sacrilege. In fact, what he has done cannot be called confession and he must repeat his confession besides accusing himself of having concealed a mortal sin from the priest through fear or through a false shame, or through any other cause.

I gave you before some reasons why you should not be afraid or ashamed to tell your sins. I will give one more reason, which is that you remember that unless you tell upon yourself, nobody in this world outside the priest, will ever know what you made known in confession. Your sins are buried forever, and your confession will never bring you into trouble or difficulty of any kind, for the priest is commanded by the Church "to take especial care, neither by word nor sign nor by any means whatever to allow, even in the least degree, any one to know what has been confessed to him in the Sacrament of Penance." No laws, no threats, no punishment will force any priest to break this law. Many confessors have suffered tortures, imprisonment, and even death rather than be unfaithful to their trust. The more then you think, the more you will be able to understand that really one of the silliest things a boy or girl can do is to keep back a mortal sin in confession. (You see I have said mortal sin because not to tell a venial sin in the sacrament would not make your confession bad.)

> One of the silliest things you can do is to keep back a mortal sin in confession.

After leaving the priest, the first thing you should do is to kneel down and thank God for the great gift He has bestowed upon you. When you have made that act of thanksgiving, then perform your penance—that is, say whatever prayers your confessor has given you to say by way of satisfaction. Do not get into the habit of putting your penance off. There is danger of your forgetting if you delay and you must remember that the performing of that penance—that is, the doing what the priest told you in confession—is an absolutely necessary part of the sacrament. Your catechism tells you this.

There is much more which I might speak of regarding confession, but you have heard enough to understand what confession is, how to make a good confession, and, above all, enough has been told you to fix in your mind one purpose and that is the purpose of never running the risk of falling into the awful sin of sacrilegious confession.

> Do not get in the habit of putting your penance off.

Some three or four months from now—or perhaps sooner—when you are preparing for your first Communion and while that time is approaching, during catechism classes—which you must never be absent from without a very good reason—you will hear still more about the Sacrament of Penance.

In the year 1726, a child was born who, when he grew up, became a Redemptorist. He is now St. Gerard Majella and the patron of a good confession. He gives courage to souls who are in danger of being overcome by fear and shame. He obtains true sorrow for those who invoke him. Therefore, go to him, my dear children, every time you are getting ready for confession, and be sure that, helped by him, your confessions will always be what God wishes them. Especially beg of him that your first confession be a perfect one.

Now, my good boys and girls, I wish you every blessing, but just now the greatest gift I can ask for you is the grace of a very good first confession.

Discussion Questions

1. Tell, in your own words or the words of Fr. Halpin, what a sin is.
2. Discuss Fr. Halpin's ideas and your own ideas of how often you should go to the Sacrament of Reconciliation.
3. Discuss again the types of contrition and which type is best. What kind of contrition do you need in order for your sins to be forgiven?
4. Have you memorized an Act of Contrition? If not, do so now. Remember to pray it each night or whenever you have need of a sin to be forgiven.
5. Review again the necessary parts of the Sacrament of Penance. Which parts are for you to do and which does the priest perform?
6. Immediately after coming out of the confessional, remember to kneel down and thank God for His gift

of mercy and forgiveness. You may wish to compose a poem or prayer for this purpose—one that you could memorize and use after each confession.

7. When should you do the penance the priest gives you? Why then?

I Talk with God

"Prayer for a Good Confession"

Saint Gerard, Patron of a Good Confession, who gave courage to souls who fear and shame had overcome; who gave sorrow to their hearts, resolution to their wills, truth to their faltering lips; help me to make a good confession. Enable me to know my sins, to be truly sorry for them, and to be firmly resolved, with God's grace, never to sin again.

Help me to confess my sins humbly and sincerely, to confess them in the spirit of faith, as confessing them to our Lord himself. Stand by me in this confession, O gentle St. Gerard, an angel of God sent to free me from sin. Amen.

"Short Act of Contrition"

O my God, I am sorry for all my sins, because they displease You, who are all-good and deserving of all my love. With Your help, I will sin no more. Amen.

Older children and adults: Memorize and pray often "The Divine Praises" as found on pages 145-146.

Lesson Seven Read-aloud Stories and Poem

The next two stories are from Fr. Lawrence G. Lovasik's *Catechism in Stories, Revised Edition,* Bruce Publishing Company, 1956, pages 71 and 253-254 respectively.

"St. Stephen Harding"

THE CISTERCIANS are a religious community whose members have given glory to the monastic life for nearly a thousand years and have never been in need of any reform. Their founder, St. Stephen Harding, was an Englishman who is as little known today as he was widely venerated during the Middle Ages. When Stephen lay dying after a heroic and holy life, he heard some of his fellow monks praising his penances and his prayer vigils.

"Surely a saint such as he need have no fears in approaching the judgment seat of God," they remarked.

"Stop your foolish talk," commanded the dying man. "I am going to God as trembling and troubled as if I had done no good at all. For if there has been any good in me, it was due entirely to the grace of God."

Application: St. Stephen Harding points out that he could not be holy without using the means God has given all of us to sanctify our souls, namely, prayer and the sacraments. The life of a Cistercian monk is one of prayer and devotion to the Blessed Sacrament—especially the Mass. Without prayer and the frequent reception of the Sacraments of Penance and the Eucharist, we cannot grow in holiness.

"The Golden Ring"

A MAN OF NOBLE RANK lived a very sinful life. Finally, touched by grace, he made up his mind to amend his life. He was too well known in France, so he went to Rome. Pope Pius VI heard his confession and was edified by the sincerity which the man showed; and yet, when it came to the penance, the nobleman said he was unable to do any of the penances the pope gave him, since his health would not permit certain sacrifices. The pope, in his wisdom, then gave him a golden ring on which were engraved the Latin words *Memento Mori*, which means, "Remember that you shall die!" The nobleman was to wear this ring and to read at least once a day the words engraved upon it.

The penance was effective. The daily sight of that ring filled the nobleman with the thought of death and he kept thinking: "If I am to die, what have I to do here on earth except to prepare for a good death? Why should I be easy on my body which will soon rot in the grave?" He kept the ring as a reminder that he should rather make atonement for his sins in this world than in the next. He led a very virtuous life, and death found him well prepared.

Application: God demands a punishment for sin. We must make up for our sins in this world or in the next. This is the purpose of the penance given in confession. The nobleman in our story is not to be imitated in his desire for a penance which suited him best. He should be imitated for his faithfulness in doing the penance that was given to him, and in using it as a means of making progress in virtue.

The following short story, "The Vision at the Confessional," comes from *Children's Retreats* by Rev. P.A. Halpin, 1926, pages 168-169.

ONE DAY a servant of God was praying in the church at a time when many people were going to confession. He saw them going into the confessional one by one, and coming out after they had made their confession.

At the same time, God opened his eyes that he might see the state of the soul of each of these people. He saw some going in whose souls seemed black and ugly; they came out white and beautiful. These were they who had gone into confession with mortal sin on their souls, and had come out forgiven.

He saw others going in black, and come out blacker and more hideous. These were the sinners who made bad confessions.

Others again he saw who entered the confessional white and beautiful, and come out shining with greater beauty and splendor. These were they who had not committed any grievous sin, but in whose souls there were venial faults; they had, by virtue of the sacramental grace given by absolution, obtained pardon for them, and an increase of grace which made them more and more beautiful before God.

———————

The following excerpts are from *The King of the Golden City Study Edition* by Mother Mary Loyola, Biblio Resource Publications, Inc., 2007, pages 65-74.

WHEN THE SOLDIERS of the King were overthrown in battle, two things happened—they were wounded more or less severely, and their white robe was sullied. If the wound was slight, the robe was soiled only. If the wound was mortal, the white robe was not only soiled but spoiled, not only spoiled but lost altogether. In both cases, the disaster came about through their own fault. They forgot either to make use of their armor, or to call for the help they needed, or they fought in a half-hearted way, so that one of Malignus' [the Devil's] well-directed blows reached a weak spot and they were hurt.

Now, was any remedy provided by the King in these circumstances? Could anything be done to cleanse or recover the white robe if it had been soiled or lost? Could any mercy be shown to a traitor, who forsaking his Sovereign King and going over to the enemy, had been mortally wounded? Surely not, you will say. But the kind King did not say so. In his Infirmary, there were costly ointments that healed even mortal wounds. There were tender-handed, tender-hearted nurses who cared for the poor patients until they were well again. The white robe, too, could be cleansed or restored, the dark stains washed away. Who would not love and try to serve faithfully a King so good and forgiving?

One reason why the King's Infirmary was always full—stretchers with the wounded were continually being carried up the steps—was that his subjects did not take the daily food he had provided for them to keep them well and make them grow up healthy and strong. They took it sometimes but not as often as he wanted. Thus, many of them were weak and sickly and gave Malignus a good chance when he came to attack them. Some came to the King's feast and saw him going around to the guests with his rich presents, or remedies for their complaints, but forgot to ask for anything when he came to them. Perhaps they did not understand that he really meant what he said when he called the food he had made ready their "daily bread." Perhaps they were not sure that he would really give them what they asked when he said, "Ask and you shall receive." Anyhow, to miss such a chance was very foolish of them, as they found out later.

———

Although the Prince Guardian was always within call whenever Dilecta was in need, and though no harm could come to her except through her own fault, he had warned her that she must watch over herself and not run into danger. More than once she had learned the hard way what comes of playing with fire.

You may have heard of the man who said to a thief, "There are two sides to my house, the inside and the outside. The inside I keep for myself, the outside I leave to you." This was the privilege of all in the Land of Exile—every man was complete master of his own house. There was no breaking in by force. The doors opened from the inside only; the windows were barred. No one could get in unless the owner let him in. Malignus could and did make himself extremely disagreeable from the outside. He could disturb, threaten, even alarm. He could come to the windows and coax and promise. But the smallest child knew that as long as those inside said, "No," he was kept outside. If people came to grief then, it was their own fault.

One day as Dilecta stood in an idle mood at the little window of her hut, thinking what a trouble it was to have to do schoolwork and do as she was told, and what a fine thing it would be to be a princess some day, she heard a soft knock at the door. I doubt if she would have heard it had she been going about her work, but as she was doing nothing, she did hear it.

Now, she knew that knock, and her Prince Guardian had told her never to listen to it but to go away from the door at once and get to work. She heard the Prince call to her; but instead of listening to him, she thought she would open the door ever so little and just peek out to see what was there. She lifted the latch. Straight-away, a great ugly foot was thrust in, and a lean hand came around the door and tried to catch her. Oh, how frightened she was!

"Prince! Prince!" she cried, "come quickly! He's push-ing so hard that I can't hold the door!"

At once, the Prince was at her side. But it was no easy matter to get the hand and foot out again.

When at last this was done, the Prince Guardian said, "You have done wrong, my child. Had you not called out at once, Malignus would have come in and hurt you dreadfully, and the King would have been angry. You must tell the King at once how sorry you are."

She met the King soon after in the wood and told him what she had done. When he saw that she was sor-ry, he forgave her.

The next time he came to the little hut and she knelt at his feet and looked into his face, she saw it was not quite the same as usual. It was grave. He did not smile nor stroke her hair. He seemed sad.

"Dear King," she said, "why don't you speak to me today? Is it because I was naughty last week? But you forgave me, didn't you?"

"I forgave you, Dilecta," he said. "I will always for-give you when you are sorry and come to me. I want you to know that because I love you so much, I am sad when you disobey me. When you hurt me, you hurt yourself too; this is what makes me sad. Though I forgive you, you have a debt of punishment to pay when you do wrong. It must all be paid before you can be let into the Golden City. I want to have you there soon, but you will have to wait outside until you have paid the debt."

"How can I pay it, dear King?"

"By trying to please me in whatever you do, by offering me the things you like to do, and by bearing patiently things you do not like—cold and hunger, hard work, disappointments and cross words—the struggle with yourself when temptation comes and your desire to be idle or disobedient, or unkind. Whenever you try to overcome Self, you are paying off your debt. It is because I want you to have it all paid before I take you away from the Land of Exile, that I let troubles come to you here. They are the money I give you to pay your debt to me. Remember this, and you will not be impatient. Know that I send them because I love you. You saw I was grave and silent today when I came into your hut. Think that you deserved it, that it will help you to pay what you owe, and you will not be discouraged or sad. Whenever I come to you, I come to help, even when I do not speak much or show all the love that is in my heart. On these days, I am giving those I love the money with which they can pay their debts."

She looked up into his face through her tears, and said softly as she took him to the door, "Have I paid some of my debt today?"

The following poem is written by Sr. Mary Josita and is from her book, *Sing a Song of Holy Things,* Tower Press, 1945, page 56.

"My Jesus, Mercy"

Dear Jesus, oh, how sad You were
The night before You died—
To think of leaving all Your friends
Without their Lord and Guide.

You knew as only God could know
The thoughts in Judas' heart.
You loved him still, and longed to see
His great, bad sins depart.

You called him "Friend," and loving looks
You gave through sad, sad eyes,
On thinking of Your coming death,
That such poor souls might rise.

I cannot see how such a man
Did not fall down and cry,
To see his Master suffering so,
And know the reason why.

I think he was so bad, and yet
I do the very same
When I add sin to sin each day
Without a thought of shame.

Oh, Jesus, here before Your feet,
I lovingly adore.
Oh, help me now to keep my word,
And never hurt You more.

Discussion Questions

1. St. Stephen Harding says, "For if there has been any good in me, it was due entirely to the grace of God." In other words, if we do a good deed, it is not us doing it but rather is our response to the grace of God. If we are viewed as pretty, we cannot be praised for that because it too is a gift from God. Our intelligence as well as our athletic and artistic abilities are also gifts of God. We can only claim our failings. How does this insight affect the examination of your conscience and your concept of sin?

2. In your own words, tell the lesson of the story, "The Golden Ring."

3. The short story, "A Vision of the Confessional," presents both good and bad examples of the use of the Sacrament of Penance. Discuss the different ways this sacrament can help or hinder our spiritual journey.

4. After reading the excerpt from *The King of the Golden City*, what resolution(s) can you make to benefit your spiritual life? What can you do to pay your "debt of punishment"?

5. In her poem "My Jesus, Mercy," Sr. Mary Josita tells us that we too often betray Jesus just as Judas did. Name some things you sometimes do that hurt Jesus.

Prayerfully read through Section VII of "A Gospel Examination of Conscience" beginning on page 153. End this session with an Act of Contrition or a prayer of your own creation.

Appendix

1. How to Prepare for the Sacrament of Reconciliation and Penance

According to the catechism of the Third Plenary Council of Baltimore (1885), in order to receive the Sacrament of Reconciliation and Penance worthily, we must

1. Examine our conscience (Make an earnest effort to recall to mind all the sins we have committed since our last worthy confession)
2. Have sorrow for our sins
3. Make a firm resolution never more to offend God
4. Confess our sins to the priest
5. Accept the penance which the priest gives us

2. Prayers

Prayer before Examination of Conscience

O, Holy Spirit, help me to know all my sins. Help me to remember that Jesus died for me. Help me to make a good confession and I promise that I will try never to sin again. Amen.

Pope Leo XIII's Prayer to St. Michael the Archangel

Saint Michael the Archangel, defend us in battle, be our protection against the wickedness and snares of the Devil. May God rebuke him we humbly pray; and do thou, O Prince of the Heavenly host, by the power of God, thrust into hell Satan and all evil spirits who wander through the world seeking the ruin of souls. Amen.

Divine Praises

Blessed be God.
Blessed be His Holy Name.
Blessed be Jesus Christ, true God and true man.
Blessed be the name of Jesus.

Blessed be His Most Sacred Heart.
Blessed be His Most Precious Blood.
Blessed be Jesus in the Most Holy Sacrament of the Altar.
Blessed be the Holy Spirit, the Paraclete.
Blessed be the great Mother of God, Mary most holy.
Blessed be her holy and Immaculate Conception.
Blessed be her glorious Assumption.
Blessed be the name of Mary, Virgin and Mother.
Blessed be Saint Joseph, her most chaste spouse.
Blessed be God in His angels and in His saints.

(Optional) *May the heart of Jesus, in the Most Blessed Sacrament, be praised, adored, and loved with grateful affection, at every moment, in all the tabernacles of the world, even to the end of time. Amen.*

3. A Gospel Examination of Conscience

Regarding the Sacrament of Penance and Reconciliation, The *Catechism of the Catholic Church* states, "The reception of this sacrament ought to be prepared for by an examination of conscience made in the light of the Word of God. The passages best suited to this can be found in the moral catechesis of the Gospels and the apostolic Letters, such as the Sermon on the Mount and the apostolic teachings[12]" (no.1454).The *Compendium of the Catechism of the Catholic Church* stresses (nos. 303 and 304) a careful examination of conscience as an essential element of the Sacrament of Reconciliation. Towards this end, each day of this retreat you are encouraged *as a family* to prayerfully read-aloud one section of the "Gospel Examination of Conscience." Prior to reading the points, it would be helpful to review the scriptural passage in question. Please briefly discuss the points of examination relative to their application to each family member's daily life.

---

[12] Consult the following texts: Matthew 5-7, Romans 12-15, 1 Corinthians 12-13, Galatians 5, Ephesians 4-6, etc.

Appendix

I. Matthew 5 (individual verses are referenced)

Do I know that everything I have—everything I am—is a gift from God? Do I accept credit for God's gifts to me? Am I too attached to the things I own? Do I spend time longing for more "things"? Do I thank God often for His gifts to me? (v. 3)

Do I get angry about sad things that happen to me? Do I complain about the crosses in my life? Do I go to Jesus for comfort when I am sad? (v. 4)

Am I impatient? Am I rude to others? Do I often defend myself to others? Do I insist on my own way? (v. 5)

Do I try to live as Jesus wants me to? Do I spend time every day in prayer? Do I try to help others live good lives? Do I stand up for what I believe? Do I defend others who are being teased? (v. 6)

Have I been mean to anyone? Do I always try to help other people? Do I try to comfort those who are sad? Do I forgive others quickly and completely? (v. 7)

Am I honest and sincere with other people? Do I love God more than anyone or anything else? Do I do good deeds for love of God (because it pleases Jesus) or so others will like me? (Are my motives pure?) (v. 8)

Do I try to make peace when others are fighting? Do I try to find compromises so all are happy? Do I try to settle disputes and disagreements between other people? Do I tease and try to make others fight between themselves? (v. 9)

Do I do the right thing even when others laugh at me? Am I kind even when others are mean? Do I give in to peer pressure because I am afraid of being teased or liked less? Do I stand up for others who are being teased or ignored? (v.10)

Am I happy and proud to be a Christian? (v.11)

Do my actions and attitudes glorify God? Do I show others by my deeds that Jesus lives in me? (v. 13-16)

Do I set a good example for others? (v. 19)

Do I get angry too easily? (v. 22)

Do I readily forgive others or do I hold grudges? (v. 24)

Do I think and act as though this life is all there is? Are all my actions and attitudes pleasing to Jesus? (v. 30)

Am I truthful in everything I say? (v.37)

Do I get angry and fight back when others are mean to me? Am I generous with my possessions? Do I willingly share with others? (v. 39-42)

Do I pray for those who are mean to me? Do I love everyone, even those who do not love or like me? Do I try to imitate Jesus in everything I do? (v. 44-48)

II. Matthew 6

Do I do good deeds just so others will notice and praise me? Am I generous to others just so they will like me? Do I call attention to the good things I say and do so others will praise me and think better of me? Do I expect to get repaid in some way for the good things I do? (v. 1-4)

Do I pray just so others will see me? (v. 5)

Do I always act as a beloved child of God should act? Do I treat God's name (and all holy names) with respect and speak them with reverence? (v. 9)

Do I try to lead others to Jesus? Do I try to set a good example of who a child of God should be? Do I try to do what I believe God wants me to do? (v. 10)

Do I receive Holy Communion as often as I can? Do I participate at Mass? Do I appreciate all the gifts and graces God gives me each day? (v. 11)

Do I tell God I'm sorry and make a good act of contrition when I have sinned? Do I tell others I am sorry when I have hurt them or mistreated them? Do I forgive others when they hurt me, or do I hold grudges? Am I kind even to those who are not kind to me? (v. 12)

Do I pray and ask my guardian angel for help when I am tempted to do something wrong? Do I let others talk me into doing things I know are wrong? Do I avoid those places and people who tempt me to do wrong? (v. 13)

Do I treat others as I want to be treated? Do I forgive others as I expect others to forgive me? (v. 14-15)

Do I insist on having or doing what I want? Do I willingly and cheerfully make sacrifices? Am I willing to let others have their way? Do I offer up my trials and crosses cheerfully to Jesus for the salvation of souls?(v. 16-18)

Am I too attached to things I own? Do I share willingly? Am I greedy? Do I think about Jesus and pray to Him often? (v. 19-21)

Am I open to what Jesus wants to teach me and what He wants me to do? (v. 22-23)

Is anything more important to me than God and the life He wants me to live? Do I think about money and things of this world more than I think about God? (v. 24)

Do I worry? Am I anxious? Do I pray for the things I need? Do I trust that God will take care of me in even the smallest matter? (v. 25-34)

III. Matthew 7

Do I judge others? Do I try to guess their motives even though I don't know them? Do I expect more from others than I expect of myself? Am I slow in realizing what I have done wrong? Do I think I am better than others? Do I make a sincere examination of conscience each day? (v. 1-5)

Do I ask God for what I want and need? Do I trust that God will answer my prayers? Do I look for the answer in unexpected places and ways, or only as I want the answer? Do I trust that He knows what is best for me? (v. 7-11)

Do I treat others as I want them to treat me? (v. 12)

Do I follow the crowd and do whatever will make me liked? Do I try to please Jesus and follow His commandments? Do I accept that being a Christian requires sacrifice? Do I try to resist peer pressure and stay true to myself always? (v. 13-14)

Do I know what Jesus and the Catholic Church teach? Am I friends with people who lead me from God and a holy life? Do I focus on doing good deeds and recognize the good deeds of others? (v. 15-20)

Do I act and have the attitude of someone who is not a Christian? Do I act as though knowing about Jesus is the same as knowing, loving, and serving Jesus? Do I value the time I spend with Jesus in prayer just as I value spending time with other friends?(v. 21-23)

Is my friendship with Jesus the most important thing in my life? Is my desire to please Him more important to me than my desire to please others or myself? Do I trust anyone (including myself) or anything in this world more than I trust Jesus? Do I rely more on worldly things to give me pleasure and peace than I do on Jesus and His Kingdom? (v. 24-28)

IV. Romans 12 and 13

Do I allow the media (TV, music, movies, magazines, etc.) or my friends to influence my decisions? Do I pray, asking God to help me understand what His will is for me? (Chapter 12, v. 1-2)

Do I ever think I am better than someone else or more important? Do I think I can take care of myself, that I don't need God or others? Do I use the gifts God has given me to their best advantage? (v. 3-8)

Is my love for others sincere? Do I love them for the right reasons? Do I truly hate all that is evil, all that is not of God? Do I always try to do the right thing? (v. 9)

Am I enthusiastic about doing what is right? Am I cheerful in my good works? Do I love others as Jesus does? Do I spread joy to others? Do I continue even when I am discouraged? Do I pray daily? (v. 11-12)

Am I generous? Am I courteous and welcoming? Am I kind to those who are not kind to me? Am I a good friend to others, happy when they are happy and considerate and consoling when they are sad? Am I friendly to everyone? Am I humble, not bragging and proud of my accomplishments? Do I think myself smarter than others? (v. 13-17)

Do I live peacefully with everyone, not teasing and picking fights? Do I forgive easily and completely? Do I try to get revenge? Am I considerate of everyone, even those who may be mean to me or unfriendly? Do I share with everyone, readily and equally? Do I try to show good example for everyone? (v. 18-21)

Do I give prompt, cheerful, and complete obedience to all who have authority over me (parents, teachers, etc.)? Do I recognize that those in authority over me take God's place? Do I respect and honor others as I respect and honor God? (Chapter 13, v. 1-7)

Do I know (and act as though I know) that love is the greatest commandment—that when I act lovingly I am fulfilling the commandments of God? Do I love others unselfishly, putting their needs before my own? (v. 8-10)

Do I act as though I understand that Jesus may come again at any time? Am I ready at any time to meet Him and be judged by Him? Do I "put on the Lord Jesus Christ" every day, allowing Him to act in me and His Light to shine through me? Can others tell by my actions that I am a Christian? (v. 11-14)

V. 1 Corinthians 13

Do I always speak lovingly? Do I boast about how smart I am or about how much I love Jesus? Do I act as though love is the highest commandment and the most important calling we followers of Jesus have? Do I always act lovingly? (v. 1-3)

Am I always patient? Am I always kind? Am I ever jealous about someone else's possessions or friends or the attention they are getting? Have I boasted or bragged? Have I been rude to others? Have I been selfish? Have I lost my temper or been quick to get angry? Have I felt sorry for myself or pouted? (v. 4-5)

Am I ever happy that someone else got in trouble? Do I put up with others cheerfully even when they are moody or hurtful? Am I forgiving to those I love and those who love me? (v. 6-7)

Am I there for others when they need me? Do I act as though how I treat others is more important to me than anything else? Do I put more value on being loving than on being smart, or being good at sports, or any other giftedness? Do I imitate the perfect love Jesus has for me in all I think, do, and say? (v. 8-13)

VI. Ephesians 4

Am I humble? Am I gentle? Am I patient? Do I bear lovingly the weaknesses and faults of others? Do I try to keep peace with everyone? (Chapter 4, v. 1-3)

Have I tried to discern the gifts God has given me? Do I use them for His glory? Do I try to grow closer to Jesus and learn more about my faith and the Catholic Church? Do I try to be loving and like Jesus in all I do? (v. 11-16)

Do I always speak the truth? Do I hang on to my anger and feel sorry for myself? Have I taken something that does not belong to me or failed to return something I have borrowed? Do I do my work honestly and to the best of my abilities? Do I share willingly with others? (v. 25-28)

Do I use bad words or curse? Do I say things that cause others to think bad thoughts or do something that is wrong?

Do I shout angry words, or do means things when I'm angry? Am I always kind to others, compassionate and understanding? Am I forgiving? (v. 29-32)

VII. Ephesians 5 and 6

Do I try to imitate Jesus in all my thoughts, words, and actions? Do I try to love others and myself as He loves us? Do I talk in any way that would offend others or Jesus? Do I thank God often for His abundant graces to me? Do I intentionally do things that are wrong, speak impurely, or act greedily? (Chapter 5, v. 1-5)

Am I friends with anyone who is a bad influence on me? Do I listen to people who speak badly about God or the Catholic Church? Do I live as a child of God, a child of the light? Do I watch carefully over how I live my life, what I say, the decisions I make? Do I try to understand and live God's will? Do I have an "attitude of gratitude"? Am I cheerfully obedient to those who have authority over me? (v. 6-33)

Do I always obey my parents cheerfully, promptly, and completely? Do I honor my parents by not speaking badly about them to others and by being considerate of their needs and wishes? Have I ever bullied or teased others? (Chapter 6, v. 1-9)

Do I ask God to help me in difficult situations and in times of temptation? Do I ask for help and protection against the Devil from God, my guardian angel, Mother Mary, and my patron saint? Do I try to stand firm in my Christian faith, fighting temptation using faith as my shield? (v. 10-17)

Do I pray often? Am I watchful over temptation? Do I ask the saints to help me become stronger in my faith? Do I speak to others about God? Do I do all I can to further the Kingdom of God on earth? (v. 18-20)

Note: For additional points of a thorough examination of conscience, you may use the Ten Commandments and the Precepts of the Church (as outlined on page 87 above), the spiritual and corporal works of mercy, the seven capital sins, any of the virtues, or the fruits of the Holy Spirit. You may also continue this exercise by devising your own points of examination from Scriptural passages not included above: Any of the Gospels or apostolic letters, such as Romans 14 and 15, 1 Corinthians 12, and Galatians 5. The book of James also provides excellent points of moral catechesis.

4. Introduction to the Practice of *Lectio Divina*

The previous "Gospel Examination of Conscience" gives us an excellent introduction to the ancient practice of *lectio divina,* which literally means "the divine reading." In this holy discipline, we dwell over a passage of Scripture, seeking not only communion with Christ but also our own radical change in Christ.

Despite its fancy name, this prayer practice is accessible to all and is similar to the procedure we used in the "Gospel Examination of Conscience." We read a short passage of Scripture, meditate on this passage in order to determine its meaning as well as its personal relevance, pray over the passage—moving the passage from the lips and mind to the heart—and contemplate its meaning with the help of divine grace.

Anyone familiar with the Little Rock Scripture Study series will see a similarity to this program's four-step Scripture reflection process: 1) *What does the Scripture passage say?* 2) *What does the Scripture passage mean?* 3) *What does the Scripture passage mean to me?* And 4) *What am I going to do about it?*

Older children and adults may begin with short Gospel passages that include the words of Christ. Deepen your prayer life with this ancient but simple prayer method.

More RACE for Heaven Products

RACE for Heaven study guides use the saint biographies of Mary Fabyan Windeatt to teach the Catholic faith to all members of your family. Written with your family's various learning levels in mind, these flexible study guides succeed as stand-alone unit studies or supplements to your regular curriculum. Thirty to sixty minutes per day will allow your family to experience:

- ☑ The spirituality and holy habits of the saints
- ☑ Lively family discussions on important faith topics
- ☑ Increased critical thinking and reading comprehension skills
- ☑ Quality read-aloud time with Catholic "living books"
- ☑ Enhanced knowledge of Catholic doctrine and the Bible
- ☑ History and geography incorporated into saintly literature
- ☑ Writing projects based on secular and Catholic historical events and characters

Purchase these guides individually or in the following grade-level packages. (Grades are determined solely on the length of each book in the series.)

Grades 3-4: *St. Thomas Aquinas, The Story of the "Dumb Ox"; St. Catherine of Siena, The Girl Who Saw Saints in the Sky; Patron Saint of First Communicants, The Story of Blessed Imelda Lambertini;* and *The Miraculous Medal, The Story of Our Lady's Appearances to St. Catherine Labouré*

Grade 5: *St. Rose, First Canonized Saint of the Americas; St. Martin de Porres, The Story of the Little Doctor of Lima, Peru; King David and His Songs, A Story of the Psalms;* and *Blessed Marie of New France, The Story of the First Missionary Sisters in Canada*

Grade 6: *St. Dominic, Preacher of the Rosary and Founder of the Dominicans; St. Benedict, The Story of the Father of the Western Monks; The Children of Fatima and Our Lady's Message to the World;* and *St. John Masias, Marvelous Dominican Gate-keeper of Lima, Peru*

Grade 7: *The Little Flower, The Story of St. Therese of the Child Jesus; St. Hyacinth, The Story of the Apostle of the North; The Curé of Ars, The Story of St. John Vianney, Patron Saint of Parish Priests;* and *St. Louis de Montfort, The Story of Our Lady's Slave*

Grade 8: *Pauline Jaricot, Foundress of the Living Rosary and the Society for the Propagation of Faith; St. Francis Solano, Wonder-Worker of the New World and Apostle of Argentina and Peru; St. Paul the Apostle, The Story of the Apostle to the Gentiles;* and *St. Margaret Mary, Apostle of the Sacred Heart*

The Windeatt Dictionary: Pre-Vatican II Terms and Catholic Words from Mary Fabyan Windeatt's Saint Biographies explains over 450 Catholic terms and expressions used in this popular saint biography series. Indispensable in expanding knowledge and practice of the Catholic faith, this book provides a ready access for the Catholic vocabulary words used in the RACE for Heaven Windeatt study guides. This dictionary also includes a Catholic book report resource that contains suggestions for forty-five Catholic book reports: fourteen writing projects, ten book report activities, and twenty-one topics for saint biographies.

Graced Encounters with Mary Fabyan Windeatt's Saints: 344 Ways to Imitate the Holy Habits of the Saints is a compilation of the "Growing in Holiness" sections of RACE for Heaven's Catholic study guides for the Windeatt saint biography series and presents 344 examples of saintly behavior, one for nearly every chapter in each of these twenty biographies. Enhance your encounter with the saints by practicing the models of devotion, service, penance, prayer, and virtue offered in this guide.

Communion with the Saints: A Family Preparation Program for First Communion and Beyond in the Spirit of St. Therese imitates St. Therese of the Child Jesus and her family who studied and prayed for sixty-nine days in anticipation of Therese's First Holy Communion. Modeling this preparation, the *Communion with the Saints* program will help any family find renewed fervor in the reception of the Eucharist. This resource includes a chapter-by-chapter study of the following four books:

- *The Little Flower, The Story of Saint Therese of the Child Jesus*—to provide the foundation of God's love for us and to encourage a desire for holiness

- *The Children of Fatima and Our Lady's Message to the World*—to show the sinfulness of our world and the need to avoid sin

- *The Patron Saint of First Communicants, The Story of Blessed Imelda Lambertini*—to inspire devotion to the Sacrament of Holy Communion

- *The King of the Golden City* by Mother Mary Loyola —to illustrate Jesus' Presence as a source of grace necessary to live a holy life

Each of the sixty-nine days of preparation includes read-aloud selections with enrichment activities, meditational readings, catechism lessons, and plenty of practical application to promote a growth in holiness and sanctity. Weekend suggestions include a list of over thirty-five family projects. The use of *My First Communion Journal* is encouraged with this program.

My First Communion Journal in Imitation of Saint Therese of the Child Jesus provides a lasting keepsake of a child's First Holy Communion. Saint Therese of the Child Jesus and her family studied and prayed for sixty-nine days prior to Therese's First Holy Communion. This journal imitates that family model of preparation for the reception of the Most Holy Eucharist. Each daily entry contains a stanza of a poem composed by Saint Therese, a quotation from Saint Faustina Kowalska's diary (*Divine Mercy in My Soul*), or a Scripture quotation. Two weekly themes—a floral theme in imitation of Saint Therese and a battle theme molded from the teachings of Saint Paul—are offered with accompanying weekly passages from Scripture suitable for memorization. This journal may be completed in conjunction with the *Communion with the Saints* program or used separately.

The King of the Golden City Study Edition is a new edition of a book that was originally published in 1921. This treasure of a book was written in response to a student's appeal for instructions along with "little stories" to help her prepare for Holy Communion. To fulfill this request, Mother Loyola of the Bar Convent in York, England, wrote a simple story that illustrates Jesus' desire to share an intimate relationship with each one of His children. This new edition contains some updated language but, quite deliberately, does not contain any pictures. Readers, as they progress through this story, will form a mental image of their King, one as unique and personal as their own relationship with Him. The study sections assist with the allegory, connect to the Bible as well as to the catechism, and explore the art of prayer in the spirit of the three Carmelite Doctors of the Church. Although written over eighty-five years ago for a young child, this book remains a timeless masterpiece of Catholic literature suitable for all ages. (Also available as a study guide only)

The Good Shepherd and His Little Lambs Study Edition is a simply told Catholic tale of four children who meet with their beloved aunt for "First Communion talks." More than a story, it is a First Communion primer that takes the tenets of the catechism and, through naturally-flowing conversations, relates them in the language of little ones to authentic Christian living. As Mrs. Bosch explains, "We might learn the catechism all the way through beautifully, and at the end find ourselves still very stiff and clumsy about loving our Lord. When He comes to us, we don't want to welcome Him into our souls only with answers out of the catechism, do we?" Enriched by appropriate Biblical passages, points of doctrine, and prayers, this story-primer is an enjoyable and effective read-aloud that will prepare the Good Shepherd's little lambs to worthily receive Him in the Holy Eucharist.

Alternative Book Reports for Catholic Students contains forty-five book report ideas to encourage critical thinking for ages seven to fourteen. These ideas are intended to provoke a reflection on those themes and topics that support and encourage Catholic living as well as some that may conflict with our Faith. Many report topics require an examination of our personal faith life and prompt us to take lessons from the saints to strengthen our own faith in God. The suggested activities vary from written exercises to creative art projects and include twenty-one topics specifically designed for saint biographies. Other activities can be used within a group or family.

Reading the Saints: Lists of Catholic Books for Children Plus Book Collecting Tips for the Home and School Library (formerly entitled *Saintly Resources*) is a valuable tool for Catholic home educators, classroom teachers, and collectors of Catholic juvenile books. *Reading the*

Saints will help you discover living books from such popular out-of-print Catholic juvenile series as Catholic Treasury, Vision Books, and American Background Books as well as current series books for young Catholics. Use this book to find:

- Over 800 Catholic books listed by author, series, reading level, century, and geographical location

- More than 275 authors of saint biographies, historical fiction, and poetry written for Catholic juvenile readers

- Publishers of Catholic children's books, present and past

- Helpful advice for collecting and caring for used books

- Hundreds of age-appropriate, accessible living books to enrich your study of the Catholic Church's rich heritage of saints and notable Catholic historical figures

- Information on how to build and maintain your own library of Catholic juvenile books

- Inspiring quotations about book collecting, reading, and the love of books

The Outlaws of Ravenhurst Study Edition contains a classic story of the persecution of Scottish Catholics that was first written in 1923 and was revised and reprinted in 1950. This 2009 edition of Sr. M. Imelda Wallace's *Outlaws of Ravenhurst* contains the revised story of 1950 plus chapter-by-chapter aids to assist readers in assimilating the book's strong Catholic elements into their own lives. The study section focuses on critical thinking, integration of biblical teachings, and the study of the virtuous life to which Christ calls us as mature Catholics. With its emphasis on virtues (theological and moral plus the gifts and fruits of the Holy Spirit), the spiritual and corporal works of mercy, and the Beatitudes, *Outlaws of Ravenhurst Study Edition* is a fun and effective catechetical tool for Catholics preparing for the Sacrament of Confirmation. (Also available as a study guide only)

The Family that Overtook Christ Study Edition: The Story of the Family of St. Bernard of Clairvaux is an excellent read for young adults who are preparing to receive the Sacrament of Confirmation. In this exciting chronicle of the life of twelfth-century knights, we have an entire family of nine saints who lay before us their individual means of achieving intimate union with Christ. Learn with the Fontaines family how to supernaturalize the natural, develop a God-consciousness, and attain sanctity by being yourself. Perfect for high-school read-aloud (or adult study), this new study edition has over 250 footnotes for increased comprehension and provides discussion/meditation points to promote the art of spiritual conversation. The appendix lists formulas of Catholic doctrine that are essential for confirmands not only to know but also to incorporate into their own spiritual lives.

A Confirmation Reader-Retreat: Read-Aloud Lessons, Stories and Poems for Young Catholics utilizes chapters from two excellent out-of-print Catholic books for children (*I Belong to God, Great Truths in Simple Stories for Children and Lovers of Children* by Lillian Clark; and *Children's Retreats in Preparation for First Confession, First Holy Communion, and Confirmation* by Rev. P.A. Halpin). This book provides a basic doctrinal review of the Sacrament of Confirmation as well as prayer experiences—a nine-day read-aloud retreat/novena. The reprinted material has been supplemented with short stories and poems that provide insights in applying catechetical doctrines to the daily life of young Catholics. Each lesson concludes with "I Talk with God"—a section that encourages readers (of all ages) to deepen their relationship with each of the Three Persons of the Blessed Trinity. Reflection questions promote the habit of spiritual conversation within your family—to encourage family members to discuss holy topics—and to help you grow together in holiness. Additionally, a traditional novena to the Holy Spirit is included.

To Order: Email info@RACEforHeaven.com or place an order from RACEforHeaven.com. Discover, MasterCard, VISA, PayPal, American Express, checks, and money orders are accepted.

www.ingramcontent.com/pod-product-compliance
Lightning Source LLC
Chambersburg PA
CBHW032101080426
42733CB00006B/365

* 9 7 8 1 9 3 4 1 8 5 3 8 4 *